Routledge Revivals

The Language Families of Africa

The Language Families of Africa

Second edition

A. Werner

Routledge
Taylor & Francis Group
Routledge Revivals

First published in 1915 by Kegan Paul, Trench, Trübner & Co., Ltd.

This edition first published in 2018 by Routledge
2 Park Square, Milton Park, Abingdon, Oxon, OX14 4RN
and by Routledge
711 Third Avenue, New York, NY 10017

Routledge is an imprint of the Taylor & Francis Group, an informa business

Publisher's Note
The publisher has gone to great lengths to ensure the quality of this reprint but points out that some imperfections in the original copies may be apparent.

Disclaimer
The publisher has made every effort to trace copyright holders and welcomes correspondence from those they have been unable to contact.

A Library of Congress record exists under ISBN: 26016186

ISBN 13: 978-1-138-60200-7 (hbk)
ISBN 13: 978-1-138-60202-1 (pbk)
ISBN 13: 978-0-429-46198-9 (ebk)

THE LANGUAGE-FAMILIES OF AFRICA

BY

A. WERNER

School of Oriental Studies (University of London); and sometime Associates' Fellow, Newnham College, Cambridge

SECOND EDITION

WITH A PREFACE

BY

SIR E. DENISON ROSS

AND A MAP

LONDON

KEGAN PAUL, TRENCH, TRUBNER & CO., Ltd.

BROADWAY HOUSE: 68–74 CARTER LANE, E.C.

1925

First Edition, 1915
Second Edition, 1925

PREFACE

PROFESSOR Werner has requested me to say a few words by way of introduction to the new edition of her *Language-Families of Africa*. And this I have much pleasure in doing, because it gives me a rare opportunity of paying a small tribute to her scholarship. Speaking as one who is quite ignorant of all African languages other than Arabic, I welcome the chance of recommending this little book to all who are interested in the history and development of human speech. Though obviously the work of a scholar who is sure of her ground and intimate with the whole field of relevant literature, Miss Werner's touch is so light and her style so simple that the little work may be read by all and sundry as an essay on the native mind of Africa, as reflected in its modes of speech. In spite of phonetic spellings and of lists of apparently unpronounceable words, it makes easy reading, and one is constantly being told strange unsuspected facts about the dark inhabitants of this vast continent, which carry the reader far beyond the interests of the mere linguist. It must not be supposed that anyone who had mastered the contents of this book would be able to express the simplest want, say, in Zulu. On the other hand, there is enough regarding the structure of the various families to show him what to look out for when he first hears a particular language spoken.

Since the first edition appeared in 1915, Sir H. H. Johnston's monumental work on the Comparative Study of Bantu has appeared: but this in no way affects the utility of the present work, which, though only intended as an elementary introduction, covers a far wider field. Some revision has been naturally found necessary, but, owing to the fact that the book was stereotyped, not much alteration was possible. A few corrections have, however, been introduced, and some notes have been added at the end, especially in connection with Chapter III. The important work of Mr N. W. Thomas and others in the field of Sudanian languages has thrown so much new light on this group that in other circumstances it might have been considered advisable to re-model this chapter. Recognition might also have been given to the important group of semi-Bantu languages. However, the importance of Prof. Werner's introduction stands, and for those who would pursue the subject further the Bibliography at the end has been entirely recast.

E. DENISON ROSS.

INTRODUCTORY NOTE ON PHONETICS IN RELATION TO AFRICAN LANGUAGES

By Daniel Jones, M.A.,

Reader in Phonetics in the University of London.

Those who have followed the recent developments in methods of language teaching will know what a prominent place is now given to *Phonetics* by our most successful teachers of the important European languages. For those, however, who are not familiar with these developments, a few remarks on the subject may not be out of place here.

Phonetics is the systematic study of pronunciation. By the aid of phonetic theory the student learns to form difficult foreign speech-sounds with accuracy, while the use of phonetic transcription helps him to learn the proper distribution of sounds in connected speech. Particulars as to the use of phonetics and its place in language teaching will be found in numerous books, and especially in Sweet's *Practical Study of Languages* (chaps. ii. to vii.), and Jespersen's *How to Teach a Foreign Language* (chap. x.). The following extracts may be quoted here. Sweet says (p. 4): "All study of language must be based on phonetics. . . . It is equally necessary in the theoretical and in the practical study of languages." Jespersen says (p. 143): "Experiment has proved to us that by means of this science we can . . . give an absolutely better pronunciation in a much shorter space of time than would be possible without phonetics;" and again (p. 176): "The use of phonetics and phonetical transcription in the teaching of modern languages must be considered as one of the most important advances in modern pedagogy."

The use of phonetic theory and of phonetic transcription in the teaching of modern languages is approved by the Board of Education. The following is a quotation from the official circular No. 797 (Memorandum on the Teaching of Modern Languages), issued in 1912 (p. 19): "The explanation of the principles of sound-production and the comparison of the sounds used in different languages are greatly facilitated by the adoption of a scheme of special symbols each of which represents one and only one sound. Many teachers go further than this, and use whole texts and books written in a phonetic script. It might seem superfluous to point out that the proper use of a phonetic script is to give training in audition and systematic practice in the reproduction of the new sounds and their combinations, while postponing for a while the further difficulty of a new and inconsistent orthography." *

Up-to-date methods have unfortunately not yet been introduced to any large extent into the teaching of African languages. † There are various reasons for this. In the first place, most of the present teachers of African languages have had little or no opportunity of studying modern methods of teaching, and they have had no phonetic training. In the second place, the pronunciation of most African languages has never been accurately analysed, the result being that it is in most cases impossible to give the student directions as to how to form the speech-sounds. Thirdly, the current orthographies of such African languages as have been

* The Appendix to this circular is particularly instructive. It contains the actual time-tables and syllabuses of the modern language instruction of several of our best schools. In all of these schools phonetics and phonetic transcription (International Phonetic system) are employed.

† A beginning is, however, being made for Arabic by the forthcoming work of Canon W. H. T. Gairdner (*Egyptian Colloquial Arabic*, to be published by Heffer, Cambridge).

written are in most cases atrocious misrepresentations of the correct pronunciation; * they effectually succeed in perpetuating our mispronunciations by concealing the difficulties.

It was therefore a source of great satisfaction to me to find that Miss Werner was insisting in this book on the value of phonetics (see p. 29 onwards). The inclusion of some specimens in phonetic transcription (pp. 51, 52, 54, 74, 80, 96, 98, 99, 114) is also a step in the right direction. It will be realized, of course, that many of these transcriptions must be regarded as tentative; further research into the pronunciation of the languages may possibly reveal errors in the transcripts and will doubtless show that improvements are possible. But in spite of possible defects, these phonetic texts serve the useful purpose of indicating the lines on which transcriptions should be made, and showing that the elaboration of a uniform system of transcription for African languages is by no means impracticable.

The system of transcription used by Miss Werner is that of the International Phonetic Association; this system is, in my opinion, the best, besides being the most widely used, of the existing phonetic alphabets. For the benefit of those to whom the system may be new it may be mentioned that it is used in several hundred books, and is almost universally adopted in England in those schools and colleges where languages are taught on phonetic principles.

D. J.

* This is the opinion I have formed after making a very minute analysis of the pronunciation of one African language (Sechuana) and a less detailed analysis of the pronunciation of several others.

CONTENTS

THE LANGUAGE-FAMILIES OF AFRICA.

CHAPTER I.

INTRODUCTORY.

Sir William Jones, who may be called the father of Comparative Philology, once put on record a remark on which the later developments of the science he originated are a curious comment. "The study of languages," he wrote, in the second volume of the *Asiatic Researches*, "has little intrinsic value and is only useful as the instrument of real knowledge."

That is to say, there is no reason—apart from the practical one of necessary communication—for learning any language which does not possess a literature. It was quite natural that Jones, whose studies were concerned with the literary languages of the East—with Persian, Sanscrit and Chinese—should hold such an opinion. It was reserved for a later generation to discover the value of *unwritten languages*, not merely for the treasures of orally-transmitted legend and folk-lore which they enshrine, but for the light which they throw on the workings of the human mind in different races and under varying conditions.

The most barbarous language is, in its degree, an instrument of human thought, and as such, worthy of a careful and reverent scrutiny. As Max Müller said long ago, "Dialects which have never produced any literature at all, the jargons of savage tribes, the clicks of the Hottentots and the vocal modulations of the Indo-Chinese are as important, nay, for the solutions of some of our problems, more important, than the poetry of Homer or the prose of Cicero."

But we must not suppose that a "barbarous" language, that is, one spoken by a barbarous or uncivilised race, is devoid of organic structure or grammatical rules. This notion is very commonly held, indeed it is implied in the very word "barbarous," which was used by the Greeks of speech unintelligible to them and therefore, it might be presumed, utterly incoherent and meaningless.

On the contrary, no language has yet been discovered which is without grammatical rules, and in many cases these rules are extremely complicated. Of course this does not mean that the rules are consciously formulated, or that there exists anything in the shape of a written grammar, unless drawn up by outsiders—by Europeans for Europeans. But if we study any one of these languages with sufficient care, we find that it proceeds according to certain fixed principles, and that the relations which we call number, gender and case are exemplified in practice by people who have never heard their names and would not understand them if they did. Thus the Rev. George Taplin * says of an Australian tribe, "The Narrinyeri do not, as an English farmer once told me he supposed they did, only make noises like beasts of the field They have a language, and a highly organised one too, possessing inflexions which ours do not. Their nouns and pronouns have three numbers—singular, dual and plural. They do not only have the cases which ours have, but several others in addition" (*i.e.* eight in all). So too, the Hottentots of South Africa, not content with the

* *Native Tribes of South Australia* (Adelaide, 1878), p. 123.

ordinary plural pronoun of the first person, have an "inclusive" and an "exclusive" plural; the former meaning "we and you" and the latter "we, but not you." Similar, and even more elaborate developments are found in Melanesia, Australia and North America.

It is only, we may say, within the last half century, that much attention has been given to African speech with a view to scientific classification. But its study for practical purposes goes back to a much earlier date. During the seventeenth century several important works, representing three of the great linguistic families with which we shall have to deal, were produced (not in every case published) by various European scholars. Wemmers (1638) and Ludolf (1651) published Dictionaries of the ancient Ethiopic language of Abyssinia. Carradori, a missionary from Pistoia, compiled a Nubian vocabulary, which remained in MS. till 1877. Müller, a Danish chaplain at the factory of Frederiksborg in West Africa, collected a vocabulary of a Gold Coast dialect, which was printed at Hamburg in 1673. The Jesuit Dias brought out his Angola Grammar at Lisbon in 1697, and another Portuguese had already produced a tract in the same language in 1643. But the most interesting of all is the attempt made by an Italian friar, Giacinto Brusciotto, to grapple with the intricacies of the Bantu languages. His little Latin book—to which we shall return in a later chapter—appeared at Rome in 1659, and is modestly entitled *Some Rules for the more easy understanding of the most difficult idioms of the People of Congo*. It is, as might be expected, expressed in terms of the Latin grammar, but the following sentence, at the very outset of his treatise, shows that he fully recognised how little these can be applied :—

"And generally, this is first to be noted, that in the present tongue we must not look for declensions, but rather principiations."

This, we might almost say, gives the keynote to the structure of the Bantu languages, as we shall see when examining them in greater detail.

At the beginning of the nineteenth century, the German traveller and naturalist, Heinrich Lichtenstein, discovered the existence of one great language-family (afterwards called the Bantu) extending from Benguela on the west coast to Kilwa on the east, including the speech of the "Cape Kafirs" and Basuto, but excluding that of the Hottentots and Bushmen. This fact was placed in a clearer light by the linguistic material collected during the next half century, and in 1869 Bleek published his *Comparative Grammar of South African Languages*, still, in spite of all deductions, a standard work.

He introduced the term "Bantu," which, though frequently objected to, is a convenient one and now so firmly established that it would be useless, even if desirable, to think of changing it. He recognised (provisionally) three families in Africa south of the Equator—the Bantu, the Hottentot and the Bushman, though too little was as yet known of the last-named to admit of its being definitely classified. It may be added that its position is not yet fully determined.

Bleek died in 1875, leaving his work still unfinished. The next scientific attempt at a classification of African languages was made by a Viennese scholar, Friedrich Wilhelm Müller, who divided them into six groups. This arrangement was followed by the late Robert Needham Cust, an Indian official who devoted the leisure of a long life to the study of languages. His *Modern Languages of Africa* (1883) was the first book to give English readers a comprehensive and systematic view of the subject, and, though it needs some correcting and supplementing here and there, still remains exceedingly useful. In fact, it is, so far, the only one of its kind.

The six divisions adopted by Müller and Cust are as follows:—

1. Semitic family.
2. Hamitic group.
3. Nuba-Fula group.
4. Negro group.
5. Bantu family.
6. Hottentot-Bushman group.

In this book, the above arrangement has been to some extent modified. The Nuba-Fula group consisted of languages which did not seem to belong to any of the other divisions, and had to be placed, provisionally, in a class by themselves, though it was doubtful how far any of them were connected with each other. They comprised Fula, spoken over a large area of West Africa; the "Nubian" languages of the Upper Nile; Masai in East Africa; Azande (Nyamnyam) and Monbutto (Mangbetu) on the northern edge of the Congo basin.

This group is now omitted, as fuller knowledge has shown that Fula and Masai are Hamitic languages, while Nuba and the rest have been placed in the Negro group.

"Hottentot" * again, has been recognised as essentially a Hamitic language; it has therefore been removed from the sixth division; but the Bushman languages (of which there are several, too distinct and important to rank as mere dialects) are retained for the present in a separate class.

The divisions are also arranged in a different order, for reasons which can be better explained a little later.

It will be noticed that two of the six divisions are called "families," while the rest are labelled "groups." It might seem superfluous to explain what a language-family is; but

* This is merely a conventional name, used for convenience. As we shall see later on, it covers several different languages, the most important of which, at the present day, is Nama.

it is better to be quite clear at the outset, and it frequently happens that people who have paid no special attention to the science of languages, find their notions on the subject very hazy.

Most European languages, including our own, are said to belong to the Aryan family of speech. When Sanscrit began to be studied in Europe towards the end of the eighteenth century—we may, for convenience, date from the foundation of the Royal Asiatic Society at Calcutta, in 1784—scholars were not only struck by the remarkable likeness between its grammar and that of the Greek and Latin languages with which they were already familiar, but recognised numbers of Greek, Latin and English words in a more or less disguised shape. Moreover, Sanscrit was found to contain ancient forms which explained the history of grammatical inflexions in European languages, and showed them to be all akin to one another, in a way unsuspected before.

This does not, of course, mean that Sanscrit was the original speech from which Greek, Latin, German, Norse and Russian were derived, but that it was a branch of some older form, whence the others also gradually grew, as the speakers travelled farther and farther in different directions from their original home.

When we say that languages are descended from a common stock, we really mean that one language has taken many different shapes in different places as time goes on. Thus, we know that, for several centuries after the Christian era, Latin was spoken throughout Italy, France, the Spanish peninsula and Northern Africa. In course of time, this spoken language (which was something very unlike the Latin we find in the classical writers) underwent considerable changes, just as spoken English was very different in Shakespeare's time from what it was in Chaucer's and has changed still further during the last three centuries.

When the Roman Empire broke up and new nations arose, each of these developed the language in its own way, so that if we like to say so, we have a number of fresh languages: Italian, French, Spanish, Portuguese, Rumanian.

But as one cannot fix any definite point of time when Latin ceased to be Latin and became Italian—or French or Spanish, as the case may be—it is perhaps more correct to say that the languages of modern Europe are various shapes assumed by Latin, than that they are descended from it. So long as this is borne in mind, however, there is no harm in using the popular metaphor which describes the original language as the mother and the others as the daughters—extending the figure to include other relationships, *e.g.*, those of sisters, first and second cousins, etc. In fact, this is often the best way of making things clear.

All languages, then, which, when their structure is examined, show such resemblances as indicate their derivation from a common stock, are called a *family* and are said to be *genetically related*. The Aryan languages, just mentioned, are such a family, the Semitic (including Hebrew, Ethiopic, ancient Assyrian, etc.) are another, so are the Bantu tongues of Central and Southern Africa. If there is no evidence of such relationship, the languages which for any reason are classed together, may be termed a group, but not a family. Müller called the class in which he placed Berber, Somali, Galla, etc., the "Hamitic group," because he did not consider their relationship to each other sufficiently clear to warrant their being entitled a family. The progress of research, however, has since shown that they are certainly connected, and we have accordingly entered them as the "Hamitic family."

In like manner, "the Negro group" seemed the only possible designation for a large number of languages, many of them very slightly known, spoken in Western and Central Africa. From the materials at the disposal of Müller and

Cust, it seemed possible to make out a few sets of related languages, but not to trace any relationship between these groups. In fact many languages had to be placed in this division for the sole reason that they were neither Bantu, Hamitic, nor Semitic.

It has now become evident, chiefly through the labours of Meinhof and Westermann, that there is a distinct family, comprising most of the West African languages (besides several others which extend in a continuous zone across the continent as far as Abyssinia), and possessing marked characteristics of its own. We therefore substitute for the name "Negro group" that of "Sudan family"* Several languages included under the old classification have been removed from this division and others (formerly placed in the "Nuba-Fula group") added to it.

We have also slightly altered the order of the divisions. The Sudan family is placed first, because it appears to be the most primitive; while it is believed by those most competent to judge that the Bantu languages are a later development, possibly arising out of the contact between Sudan and Hamitic speech. We therefore place the Bantu family second and the Hamitic third, followed by the Bushman language, which for the present at any rate, it is desirable to treat separately. The Semitic family comes last, because it is not really indigenous to Africa. We cannot, indeed, be certain that the other languages—the Hamitic ones at any rate—originated in Africa; but, if not, we do not know when they came in, whereas we do know when Punic and Arabic did.†

Languages, again, are classed, not only according to

* "Sudan" or "Sudanian" in this connection is preferable to "Sudanese," because this last, in Egypt and East Africa, has acquired a special and restricted meaning.

† The Semitic languages of Abyssinia are, perhaps, an exception. They probably came in from Arabia at a very early date, but it is not known when this happened.

relationship, or *genealogically*, but also *morphologically*, that is, according to their structure, or, as Tucker puts it, "the formation of words and particularly the modifications involved in what is known as declension or conjugation, or more comprehensively as *accidence*."

Most philologists are agreed that there are three distinct types of language: the *Isolating*, the *Agglutinating* and the *Inflexional*.

1. In *Isolating* languages, such as Chinese and some West African idioms (Tshi, Ewe, etc.), all words are monosyllables * and undergo no modification to express person, gender, number, case, mood or tense. All syntactical relations have to be shown by the order of words in a sentence. As there are no words of more than one syllable there is no such thing as *word-stress*, or "*accent*": † its place is taken by *intonation* or *pitch*.

2. In the *agglutinating* languages, so-called *formative elements* are attached to the *roots* in order to express relations of number, case, tense and so forth. (In words such as "god-like," "white-ness," "wise-ly," "house-s," "child-ren," "love-d," "up-lift," *god, white, wise, house, child, love, lift*, are the roots, the rest of each word is a *formative element*). But, in agglutinating languages, the formative elements can always be recognised as independent words detachable from the root, which can be affixed to other roots, or even stand alone in the sentence. Thus we have in Turkish *sev-ish-dir-il-me-mek*, "not to be brought to

* This requires some qualification, as will be explained in the chapter on the Sudan languages.

† By "stress" is meant the strong force of breath with which one particular syllable in a word is pronounced, *e.g.*, in English, German, Italian, etc., as *gár-den, contáin, Fénster, cam-mí-no*, etc. "Pitch" (the voice going up or down on a syllable) will be discussed later; it is enough to say here that it has a very important function in the isolating languages, since, the number of syllables being limited, the same word has to be used in several different sentences, which can only be distinguished by the varying intonations—the "tones" which form such a difficulty in learning Chinese.

love one another," "where *sev* means 'love' and each of the following syllables has its separate and separable meaning" (Farrar).* Such words, in fact, are formed on the same principles as some of the English ones quoted just now ("god-like," "up-lift," etc.), only the principle is carried to a much greater length.

3. The *Inflexional* languages (also called "organic" or "amalgamating") resemble the last-named in having formative elements added to the root, but they are no longer recognisable as separate words and cannot be used apart from it. Compare the *-ly* in "manly," the *-d* in "loved," the *-ness* in "goodness," etc. Moreover, as Professor Meinhof says, "they modify the meaning of words not merely by prefixes and suffixes, but by internal change of vowel," such a change as we find in "man, men," "foot, feet," "sing, sang, sung," etc.†

It should be added that the inflexional languages alone recognise the distinction between masculine and feminine; the others have no grammatical gender in our sense, though they may have other distinctions which will be mentioned later.

It must be borne in mind that no hard and fast boundary lines can be drawn between these three classes. At one time it was thought that they constituted fixed and unchangeable divisions; no isolating language could ever become agglutinating, and no agglutinating language inflexional. Other philologists maintained that there were not three different kinds of language, but three stages which every language must pass through in the order given above. This view appears to be nearer the truth than the other, but it must not be pressed too closely. We have proof that

* *Language and Languages*, p. 392.

† This, in European languages, is called *Ablaut.* For the way in which it is produced, see Whitney, *Language and the Study of Language*, p. 80.

development has taken place—in some instances we can see it going on under our eyes—and, very often, the tendency is not to acquire inflexions, but to shed them (as in modern English and in Cape Dutch) and so reduce polysyllables to monosyllables.

What we can say for certain is, that many languages whose main tendency is isolating have agglutinative features; some agglutinating languages show traces of inflexion; and sometimes it is doubtful in which class any particular language ought to be placed. The Bantu languages are commonly called agglutinating, yet many of their formative elements are true inflexions, which cannot be used apart from the root. English, through shedding its inflexions, as we saw just now, has become to a certain extent isolating and gives no indication whether a noun is subject or object; in a sentence like "the dog bit the man" you can only tell by the order of the words that it was not the man who bit the dog. Then, again, words like "godlike," "undertake," "overturn," are formed on the agglutinative principle, but the termination *-ly* (a contraction of *like*, as in "godly") is a true inflexion and cannot stand alone. Most of our formative elements can be recognised as the worn-down remains of complete words.

The whole matter is put very clearly in the fourth, fifth and sixth chapters of Dr. Tucker's *Introduction to the Natural History of Language*, which is one of the best books available for obtaining a general view of the subject.

Coming back to the five divisions under which African languages are grouped for the purposes of this book, we find them to stand as follows :—

1. The Sudan family. Isolating.
2. The Bantu family. Agglutinating.
3. The Hamitic family. Inflexional.
4. The Bushman group. Doubtful at present.
5. The Semitic family. Inflexional.

CHAPTER II.

THE FIVE FAMILIES OF AFRICAN LANGUAGES.

We will now take a brief survey of these five groups, reserving the detailed treatment of each for future chapters.

I. The Sudan family extends from Cape Verd to Abyssinia and comprises probably over two hundred languages, while fresh ones are continually being brought to light. Among the best known are Shilluk, on the Upper Nile, Gang ("Acholi") in the Uganda Protectorate, Tshi and Gã (Gold Coast), and Kunama (Abyssinia).

Their main characteristics are—

Monosyllabic basis. (This does not necessarily mean that all the words are of one syllable; but the point will be discussed in the next chapter.)

Absence of grammatical gender and of all inflexions.

The use of Intonation or Pitch for distinguishing words.

Position of the Genitive (or Possessive Case); the possessor always precedes the thing possessed. We can say in English, "the man's house," or "the house of the man." The Gold Coast native can only say "the man's house" (or, rather, "man house": there is no article and nothing corresponding to the *'s* which is our possessive inflexion).

Where words are all of one syllable, there can, naturally, be no such thing as accent, or word-stress.* Even when

* Sentence-stress, which is variable (*cf.* the different ways of accenting "How do I know?" according to the idea most prominent in the mind of the speaker), is an entirely distinct matter.

several monosyllabic words are compounded into one, there is no special stress on any—the accent being evenly distributed. But each syllable has its own pitch, whether high, low, rising, falling or level; and this, as we saw before, is a means of distinguishing between otherwise identical syllables.

Very often, no difference is made between the singular and plural nouns; sometimes there is what looks like a plural inflexion, but it is a separate word—perhaps the pronoun "they," or some word meaning "men," "people," etc. Where, as sometimes happens, this word is disguised by contraction, it is difficult to draw the line between an isolating and an agglutinating language.

II. Professor Meinhof thinks, as we shall see later on, that the Bantu languages were developed out of I. under the influence of Hamitic (or pre-Hamitic) speech. Geographically, they come next to the Sudan languages, the border-line being, in many places, very ill-defined, as, for instance, in the northern part of the Congo basin. The Bantu extend over the whole of Africa south of the Congo and Lake Victoria, reaching up to the Tana river on the eastern side of the continent; but their area is not quite continuous, being interrupted by islands or "enclaves" of Masai and Galla in the east, "Hottentots" in the south, and a few other tribes or fragments of tribes elsewhere.

The main peculiarities of the Bantu languages are—

Inflexion by means of prefixes (or, as Brusciotto says, "principiation instead of declension").

Absence of grammatical gender.

The alliterative concord.

There are well known examples of the use of prefixes in the names of the countries, tribes and languages. Thus, M-Swahili, Mo-sutu, Mu-giryama, Omu-ganda indicate, respectively, one individual belonging to these tribes, the plural form being Wa-Swahili, Ba-sutu, A-giryama, Aba-ganda, while the language is Ki-Swahili, Se-sutu, Lu-ganda and the country (this formation is not found everywhere), Le-sutu, Bu-ganda, U-sambara, etc.

Not only the plural of nouns is indicated by prefixes, but the agreement of adjectives, and the person, tense, etc., of verbs. Most European languages, as we know, make these changes either by means of *suffixes*, *i.e.*, letters or syllables added at the end of a word (" town-s," " love-d," " high-er "), or by vowel-gradation (*Ablaut* and *Umlaut*). Suffixes are not altogether absent from the Bantu languages, being used to indicate certain forms and moods of the verb (*e.g.*, the causative, the subjunctive, some of the negative tenses), and, in some, the diminutive, the locative, etc. Moreover, there are certain changes governed by what is called the " Law of Vowel-Harmony," the vowel of the suffix being determined by that occurring in the body of the word. But the prefix-formation is so marked and so prevalent that it may be called the most salient characteristic of the language.

There is no distinction of masculine and feminine; it is not merely that nouns have no feminine terminations, but there are not even separate pronouns corresponding to " he " and " she." There is, however, a set of distinctions quite strange to us, nouns being divided into a number of classes (usually eight or nine) distinguished by their prefixes. One of these classes, having for its prefix in the singular some form of **umu**, and in the plural some form of **aba**, contains the names of persons (as, *e.g.*, in Zulu **um-fazi**, " a woman," **aba-fazi**, " women," **um-lamu**, " brother-in-law," plural **aba-lamu**). One consists of verbal nouns, having the prefix **ku**; one contains abstract nouns, and one (among other things) the names of trees; but in general it is difficult, if not impossible, to find a clear and consistent definition of any but the person-class and the *ku*-class.

Some think that these classes were a primitive arrangement which, in some languages, ultimately gave rise to what we understand by gender; we shall have something to say on this point in our fifth chapter.

The prefix of each class is attached, in some form or other, to all words agreeing with any noun of that class. Just as in Latin we have *bon-us domin-us, bon-a domin-a,* so we find in Zulu **um-fazi omu-hle**, in Swahili **m-toto m-zuri**. The root of the word (**-fazi, -hle, -toto, -zuri**) always remains unaltered, the prefix changes; the plural of the above words would be **aba-fazi aba-hle, wa-toto wa-zuri**. Besides this, the prefix re-appears as a pronoun attached to the verb: **um-fazi omu-hle u-ya-sebenza,** "the good woman she works," where the **u** represents both the pronoun "she" and the final *-s* of the English. (Bantu sentences are always like this: "the man *he* goes," "the rain *it* falls," etc., the verb must not follow its noun direct, without a connecting pronoun, and this connecting pronoun can never stand alone. There are other pronouns which can stand alone, but they must never be put directly before the verb-root.)

The prefix of the person-class, then, will, generally speaking, be the pronoun corresponding to "he" or "she" as the case may be. There are as many different words for "they" as there are classes, and as many words for "it" as there are classes outside the person-class.

This reappearance of the prefix before every word in agreement with the noun is called the *Alliterative Concord*. Taken strictly, this would mean that all the words in question begin with the same sound; in practice this is not always the case, the form of the prefix being subject to variation (we see this even in the Zulu sentence given above), but the same sound recurs to such an extent that the name is apt enough.

The greater number of formative elements in Bantu

are (like the pronouns mentioned above) inseparable and cannot be used by themselves, though it is often quite easy to recognise them as derived from independent words. And as we sometimes even find cases of internal vowel-change (see above, p. 18), such as the perfect of some verbs in Zulu, *e.g.*, **lele** from **lala, pete** from **pata,** it seems as though these languages should be called inflected, or at least on the way to become so, rather than agglutinating.

Most Bantu languages have a marked word-stress usually on the last syllable but one (penultimate) * as **Mu-gán-da, o-mú-hle.** Pitch accent is found to a great extent in some of them, in others it would seem to be absent, or comparatively unimportant, though it is very hazardous to assume, without careful investigation, that such is the case. It should also be noticed that all syllables end in a vowel, so that we must divide **u-mfa-zi**—not **um-fa-zi,** as written above in order to mark the division between prefix and root. Except in combinations with *m, n* and ŋ (written in many books *ṅ* or *ng'*) (which are very common, as may be seen in such place-names as Mbweni, Ngomeni, Ntumbi, etc.), it is very rare to find one consonant following another without a vowel between.

The position of the genitive differs from that usual in the Sudan languages; the *thing possessed* always comes first, "the house of the man," not "the man's house." *Of* is expressed by the particle **-a,** which takes an initial letter according to the class of the noun it agrees with.

Thus in Zulu—

Aba-ntwana b-a lo' mu-ntu.
(The) children of this person.

But **Izi-ndhlu z-a 'bantu.**
(The) houses of (the) people.

The order of words in the sentence, however, is the same

* This, at any rate, is *in general* the most prominent accent. We shall return to this point in Chapter IV.

in both families: subject, verb, object; as it usually is in English: "The man builds the house," etc.

The Bantu family seems to contain as many languages as the Sudan—possibly more.* Over three hundred names have been recorded; and, though some of these may have to disappear on closer examination, as being those of mere dialects, or different names for the same language, yet, on the other hand, fresh ones are continually being added to the list.

It is a remarkable fact, to which we must recur again later on, that some languages, apparently belonging to the Sudan family and originally without prefixes, seem to be in course of acquiring them. This is known to be the case with Mbugu, the speech of a small isolated tribe in German East Africa; perhaps it is also taking place in some parts of the Congo basin.

III. The Hamitic family once extended in an unbroken area right across North Africa. The ancient Egyptians spoke a Hamitic tongue, so did the Libyans and Numidians, whose descendants are now known as Berbers and Kabyles. Wedges were driven into this area by the Greek Colony of Cyrene and the Phœnician one of Carthage, and, later on, by the Roman occupation; while, on its southern fringe, many Hamitic peoples have been broken up and scattered. Sometimes they have been forced in among a negro population and mixed with them to such an extent that the contact has influenced their language, as has happened to the Hausa, Nandi and Masai.

All the Hamitic languages are very fully inflected and possess grammatical gender, the most usual sign of the

* Herr Struck's enumeration is as follows:—

Sudan: 264 languages + 114 dialects.
Bantu: 182 languages + 119 dialects.

I am inclined to think that the latter estimate is too low, but something depends on the definition of a dialect.

feminine being **t.** Besides those already mentioned, some of the principal ones are Somali, Galla, Saho (near the Red Sea), Fula (which, though classed with this family, in some respects stands quite by itself), Nama and other languages of the so-called "Hottentots." *

The position of the genitive is the same as in Bantu, but the order of words is different; the verb usually (not invariably) precedes the subject.

Hamitic speech has one remarkable characteristic, which has been called the *Law of Polarity*. This will be discussed in the fifth chapter; for the present it is enough to say that one of the ways in which it works is for nouns masculine in the singular to take feminine terminations in the plural and *vice versâ*.

IV. *The Bushmen*—the earliest inhabitants of South Africa of whom we have any knowledge—have now all but disappeared from Cape Colony, but are still to be found in the Kalahari Desert and in some parts of the Transvaal. There are a number of different tribes, speaking quite distinct languages. These seem to have some characteristics in common with the Sudan family; but the peculiar click-sounds, of which there are six, if not more, are not found elsewhere except among the Hottentots and (possibly) the Sandawi in East Africa, of whom very little is known. (The clicks in Zulu were borrowed from the Hottentots). There was formerly a notion current that it was impossible for any European to acquire the Bushman language, but some of its dialects were successfully studied by the late Dr. Bleek and his sister-in-law, Miss Lucy Lloyd; we

* This ridiculous appellation, now too firmly rooted to be dispensed with, is not the name of any tribe, but a nick-name applied by the early Dutch settlers to the natives they found at the Cape, who, they said, spoke no intelligible language, only an absurd gibberish which was nothing but "hot" and "tot." The tribes who have kept their own language are the Namaqua and Korana; the rest have ceased to speak anything but Cape Dutch or an equally corrupt form of English.

understand that the Rev. S. S. Dornan, of Johannesburg, has collected a number of words and phrases from the Masarwa tribe; and a German missionary, Mr. H. Vedder, has published an outline grammar of the Kung language, spoken in the neighbourhood of the Okavango river.

V. The principal Semitic language in Africa is Arabic, which came in with the Muhammadan conquerors in the seventh century, and is now spoken throughout Egypt and North Africa, though it has not quite displaced the native Hamitic speech in Algeria and Morocco. Another Semitic language, now quite extinct, is Punic, spoken by the Tyrian colonists who founded Carthage. Ethiopic, or Ge'ez, the old language of Abyssinia (still used in the liturgies of the Abyssinian Church) and its descendant, Amharic (though some scholars appear to entertain a doubt about the latter), are also Semitic, as well as Harari and three or four minor languages of Abyssinia.

The Semitic languages are very fully inflected—by prefixes, suffixes, and vowel-changes in the body of the word (*Ablaut*). Their outstanding feature, distinguishing them sharply from the Hamitic family (with which they have otherwise much in common), is the existence of the *triliteral roots* which play so large a part in Hebrew and Arabic grammar. The ground-form of the verb is the third person singular of the perfect tense, and this usually consists of three consonants, as in Arabic—*nasara* "he helped," *kataba*, "he wrote," etc. Grammatical gender is marked, not only in nouns, adjectives and pronouns, but even in the second and third persons of verbs.

Unlike all the languages previously mentioned (except some belonging to the Hamitic family) these possess written characters; indeed we owe our own alphabet (which came to us through the Romans) to the Phœnicians. The Arabic writing, imported into Africa by the early conquerors and colonists,* was long ago brought into use for both Swahili and Hausa ; but the great mass of African speech has, up to a comparatively recent date, remained unwritten and been transmitted by word of mouth only.

European missionaries—usually the first to reduce a language to writing—have introduced the Roman alphabet into their schools, adapting it as well as they could to the sounds of native speech. The result has often worked fairly well in practice, *e.g.*, the method of writing Swahili introduced by the late Bishop Steere, though it disregarded some of the finer shades of pronunciation. But (1) some languages have sounds—the very difficult ones are not, after all, numerous—unprovided for in the Roman alphabet, though its three superfluous letters, *c*, *q*, *x*, have sometimes come in usefully, as in Zulu ; and (2) for scientific purposes, not only the greatest attainable exactitude, but some degree of uniformity is desirable, and at present nearly every mission has a different system of spelling—some of them cumbrous and even misleading. Then, too, we find various observers adopting different equivalents for the same sound. There is an enormous difference between individuals, in sensitiveness of hearing and in the accuracy with which impressions are registered, and even a fairly well-trained linguist learns to distrust his own ear when dealing with unfamiliar sounds.

This is where the value of *phonetics* comes in. If we know exactly how a sound is produced, the position of the tongue, the use made of lips, teeth, etc., the extent to which the mouth is opened, and so on, we are on firm ground, even when we cannot be quite certain what the sound is

* The Arabs began founding settlements on the East Coast towards the end of the seventh century, the oldest, Pate, being said to date from 689. Swahili is spoken by the mixed race descended from these colonists and the Bantu natives. It is a purely Bantu language in structure, though it has incorporated many Arabic words into its vocabulary.

when we merely hear it. This is just what the new science of phonetics enables us to do, and it is a good sign that missionaries and others whose work entails the learning of unwritten languages, should be availing themselves more and more of the training which it affords.

Having determined the sounds, the next question is the method of writing them, and of course it is highly desirable that the method should be uniform, in order to save time and labour in learning, to facilitate comparison between different languages and to make results easily accessible to British and Continental scholars alike.

An attempt in this direction was made, some fifty years ago, by Lepsius, with his "Standard Alphabet," which was adopted by missionary societies in various parts of the world, but speedily proved its imperfection by giving rise to at least six different systems. It has been remodelled on sound phonetic principles and greatly improved by Professor Meinhof of Hamburg, and in this form it is largely used by German missionaries and other linguistic students. It is, perhaps, open to some objections which I need not discuss here; the greatest of all is the impossibility of making it universal in this country, and, that being so, the effort to introduce it at all seems little better than a waste of labour.

It is impossible that any system should be perfect; it is essential that it should be capable of improvement and that there should be some reasonable prospect of getting it generally accepted. The script of the *International Phonetic Association*, if not absolutely ideal, goes a long way towards solving the difficulty. Its framers have succeeded in finding satisfactory symbols for all the new sounds that have been phonetically determined, while the determination of those as yet unrecorded is being carried out, as opportunity allows, with the greatest care and accuracy.

A table of the International Phonetic script is subjoined.

The specimen texts appended to Chapters III., IV., V. and VI. will, as far as possible, be given in this as well as in the ordinary spelling used for the language in question.

As this is not a treatise on Phonetics (the reader is referred to the books enumerated in the Bibliography, which, however, are of little assistance unless supplemented by a course of lectures), the following notes contain only what is absolutely necessary in order to make use of the table.

Plosive sounds (also called "stops," or in older books "mutes") are produced by the *complete* closure of both mouth and nose-passage. For *nasals*, the mouth-passage is blocked, but the breath is allowed to escape through the nose. For *Fricatives* ("spirants" or "continuants") the mouth-passage is not completely blocked, but some breath is allowed to escape through a narrow opening; while for vowels, it is quite open, though in different degrees. The first column of the table shows the *mode* of *articulation*, beginning with the complete closure (the *plosive*) and ending with the most open of the vowels—**ɑ**. The cross-divisions of the table indicate the *place* of *articulation*, beginning with the lips (**p, b**) and ending with the larynx (the glottal stop, **ʔ**, and **h**). Nearly all consonants occur both *breathed* or *voiceless* (**p, t, k**) and *voiced* (**b, d, g**); these terms are now generally used instead of "hard" and "soft" or "surd" and "sonant." Of the pairs of sounds printed in the table, the *first* is the voiceless, the *second* the voiced. *Alveolar* sounds are those produced by pressing the tongue against the "teeth-ridge" or "upper gums," like our English **t** and **d**, whereas French **t** and **d** are strictly dental—formed with the tongue against the teeth. The term *retroflex* is applied to the sounds in some books called "cerebral," which are produced by turning back the tip of the tongue and pressing it against the hard palate. Many Bantu languages have a **t** and **d** produced in this way, in

		Bilabial.	Labio-dental.	Labio-alveolar.	Labio-velar.	Dental.	
CONSONANTS.	Plosive	p b					
	Plosive - Fricative		pf bv	tσ dϱ	px bg		tɬ
	Nasal	m					
	Rolled..........						
	Fricative........	ꜰ ʋ	f v	σ ϱ	ʍ† w	θ ð	ɬ
VOWELS.	Close. Half-close. Half-open. Open.						

~ nasalization. ː length. ʹ stress

ʼ closed glottis.

Meinhof's notation partly coincides with the above. The principal

ꜰ = f̱	ϱ = z̬	tɬ = ṱ	ʒ =
ʋ = v̱	θ = s̭	ɬ = s̬	ʎ =
σ = s̬	ð = z̭	ʃ = š	c =

Sounds for which Meinhof gives no equivalent are marked in has a "velar-labial" m̑h and "inter-dental" t̯, d̯, n̯, l̯, also χ̌, found sound," produced by "raising the middle of the tongue to the soft

Alveolar-lateral.	Alveolar Front.	Alveolar Back.	Cerebral.	Palatal-lateral.	Palatal.	Velar.	Uvular.	Laryngal
	t d		ṭ ḍ		c ɟ	k g	q ɢ	ʔ
dl	ts tz	tʃ dʒ		cʎ̥ ɟʎ	cç ɟj	kx gg		
	n		ṇ		ɲ	ŋ		
	r		ṛ				ʀ	
l̥	s z	ʃ ʒ		ʎ̥† ʎ	ç j	x g	ʁ̥† ʁ†	h† ɦ
					Front. i ɪ e ɛ a	Back. u ʊ ə o ʌ ɔ ɑ		

(placed immediately before stressed syllable).

differences are as follows :—

= ž	ɟ = dj	ç = χ́	ɢ = ḡ
= l′	ɲ = ń	x = χ	ɦ = h
= tj	ŋ = ṅ	g = γ	ʔ = ’

the Table with a †. In addition to the sounds in the Table, Meinhof in some Bantu languages, and described as a "velar with hushing palate and sending the breath out against the lower teeth."

[*To face p.* 30.

addition to dental or alveolar sounds—some appear to have all three.

Palatal sounds are those "articulated by the front of the tongue * against the hard palate" (Jones).

Velar consonants are those produced with the *back* of the tongue against the soft palate, or velum.

Uvular sounds (which do not occur in Standard English) are produced by means of the *uvula*, which is a prolongation of the soft palate.

Glottal sounds are produced in the glottis, which is the interval between the vocal chords.

ꜰ, ʋ, are very common sounds in African languages; they do not occur in English, but **ʋ** is found in Spanish and in some German dialects. **ꜰ** is the sound made in blowing out a candle. Ordinary **f** and **v** (as may be seen by pronouncing "fan" "van,") are formed by placing the lower lip against the upper teeth; **ꜰ** and **ʋ** are similar sounds, produced with both lips. The "labio-alveolar fricative" σ is peculiar to some of the south-eastern Bantu languages, *e.g.*, in the Thonga word *vuσa* = "bread." It has been written **sw, ps** and **ŝ** and can be imitated by putting the mouth in the position to pronounce θ (**th** in "*thin*") and then rounding the lips strongly. M. Junod compares it to the whistle produced by blowing into a key. θ is **th** in "*thin*," ð the corresponding voiced sound (**th** in "*then*"); tɬ, ɬ and dɮ are peculiar sounds found in Zulu, Chwana and Thonga, and usually called "laterals": ɬ (equivalent to the Welsh **ll** in "*Llewellyn*") is the voiceless sound of **l**, with added friction. The corresponding voiced sound occurring in Bantu is a strongly fricative variety of l.
sound occurring in Bantu is a strongly fricative variety of **l**.
Professor Meinhof, following Endemann, regards these "laterals" as quite distinct from the ordinary **l** sounds.

* By this is meant the middle part of the tongue, which when at rest is opposite the hard palate. The part opposite the gums is called the *blade*.

and thinks that they are all articulated at one point between the palatal and retroflex sounds.

ʍ, the voiceless sound of **w** in "*watch*," is heard in our Northern English pronunciation of "*which*," "*when*," etc.

ʃ is **sh** in "*shire*"; ʒ the corresponding voiced sound (**z** in "*azure*"; French **j** in "*jeune*").

ʎ is the Southern French "*l mouillé*"; Italian **gl** in "*egli*."

c, ɟ, are sounds approaching to **ty, dy,** but intermediate between these and **ky, gy.** See *Principles of the International Phonetic Association*, 1912, § 43.

ç is German **ch** in "*ich*," the voiced sound of which is English y in "*yes*."

σ, see p. 27, ϱ is the corresponding voiced sound.

ɲ is the sound of **gn** in the French "*ignorer*" (= Spanish **ñ** or Portuguese **nh**).

ŋ is the sound of **ng** in "*sing*"; in Bantu texts often written **ng'** or **ñ**. (The latter symbol should be got rid of, if possible.)

x is **ch** as found in Scots and German ("*ach*," not "*ich*").

ɡ the corresponding voiced sound.

q is the Arabic *qaf* (ق) a sound similar to **k**, but produced farther back.

ɢ the corresponding voiced sound.

ʀ is "the uvular **r** heard in Northumberland and in many parts of France, etc."

ʁ represents a variety of ʀ produced in the throat. It is one kind of Parisian ʀ, also the Arabic غ (usually transliterated *gh*, though at Cairo this is pronounced as ɡ).

ʔ indicates the "glottal stop,"* not existing in present-day Standard English, but found instead of **t** in many dialects of English, especially in Scotland. It is also a common sound in German, being exemplified in the correct pronunciation of such a word as *Verein*, which English

* See Jones, *Pronunciation of English*, pp. 16, 18.

people are apt to divide as if the **r** belonged to the second syllable (*Ve-rein*), whereas it should be *Ver-ein*, with a slight, but distinct pause after the **r**. This sound (the Arabic *hamza*) is especially characteristic of the Semitic and Hamitic languages and is also found in combination with other consonants, which are thus written **p'**, **t'**, **r'**, etc.

h is the ordinary voiceless aspirate, as in English "house."

ɦ is voiced **h**.

CHAPTER III.

THE SUDANIAN FAMILY.

LEPSIUS, writing before 1880, divided all African languages into three classes—

1. Semitic.
2. Hamitic.
3. Primitive African { A. Bantu. B. Mixed Negro.

The difference between 3 A and 3 B was, he thought, that B had no prefixes, while, as it also had no grammatical gender, it could not be included in either 1 or 2.

Substantially the same classification was adopted by Friedrich Müller and Cust, who used the term "Negro Group," as a provisional name, implying no theories as to the mutual relationship of the languages in question. "Friedrich Müller states that there is sufficient evidence to prove beyond doubt that the languages recorded in this field cannot be derived from a common Mother-Speech, but must have distinct seed-plots" (Cust). At that time, and with the materials at his disposal, he could hardly come to any other conclusion.

Now, however, that a greater number of these languages have been more or less thoroughly examined, it becomes evident—

(1) That several have to be removed from the group, *e.g.*, Hausa, Masai, and Bari, which are now found to be Hamitic.

(2) That the remainder are genetically connected, *i.e.*, can be shown to descend from one common original.

This important discovery was made by Professor Westermann, one of the lecturers at the Berlin Oriental Seminary, who had spent several years as a missionary in West Africa and become familiar with Ewe,* one of the most typical Sudanian languages, of which he has published an excellent Grammar and Dictionary.

On returning to Europe, he continued his linguistic work, in collaboration with Professor Meinhof, and gradually became convinced that Ewe shared its principal characteristics, not only with Tshi, Gã and Fanti, its near neighbours, but with Ibo and Nupe on the Lower Niger, Teda (" Tibbu ") north of Lake Chad, and even with Dinka on the Upper Nile and Kunama in Abyssinia. It may be said that the way was paved for a similar conclusion by the late Colonel Ellis, who pointed out, to begin with, the relationship between Ewe, Tshi and Gã, and by Sir H. H. Johnston, who, more recently, worked out a further series of connections; but this does not diminish the credit due to Westermann for what may be called an important step in advance.

In his book, *Die Sudansprachen* (1911), on which this chapter is to a great extent based, he examines five West African languages and three from East Africa. The former are Tshi † (Gold Coast), Gã (Accra, in the eastern part of the Gold Coast Colony as far as the River Volta), Ewe (Gold Coast east of the Volta, Togo and Dahome), Yoruba (the hinterland of Badagry and Lagos), and Efik, in the Delta of the Cross River. The languages chosen

* Variously spelt Ewe, Eʻwe (Ellis), Efe, Ephe, and Eve. The consonant is really "bilabial v," written by the Phonetic Association ʋ and by Meinhof v̱ : so that the spelling Ewe (though here adopted for convenience) is not strictly correct.

† Also written Twi, Tshwi, Tji. The real sound of the medial consonant seems to be that of σ (see p. 27), but for the purposes of this book the form "Tshi" has been retained.

from East Africa are Kunama, Dinka and Nuba (or Nob), spoken by the Nubians in the region of the Nile Cataracts and in Dongola.

The locality of these eight languages is roughly indicated on the map.

The Sudanian speech-group thus reaches in an irregular band right across Africa, from Cape Verd on the west to the confines of Abyssinia on the east, with several outlying patches (enclaves) isolated among the languages of other families, such as Kunama, in the north of Abyssinia, Nyifwa (usually called "Nilotic Kavirondo") at the north-eastern corner of Lake Victoria, and Mbugu, spoken by a small tribe of herdsmen in German East Africa. This last is particularly interesting, for a reason already referred to.

What, then, are the characteristics which these languages have in common? We may put them briefly thus:

> Monosyllabic basis.
> Absence of Inflexions.
> Genitive placed before its governing noun.

None of these points must be taken *absolutely*; we have already seen that we rarely get a language of perfectly pure type, an isolating one which does not show the beginnings of agglutination, or an agglutinating one which has no real inflexions; while the inflexional type of speech frequently tends to revert to the isolating. But, broadly speaking, we find that the *general tendency* of the Sudanian languages is to exhibit the above three features; and, in stating the subject in outline (which is all that we can attempt to do here) we shall not take into account—beyond occasionally indicating their existence—the exceptions and cross-currents which we are sure to encounter as soon as we take up the detailed study of any particular language.

The want of grammatical gender (which has not been mentioned separately, the other inflexions being likewise absent) is a feature which the Sudanian languages have in common with the Bantu. But the latter do, as we shall see in the next chapter, indicate other grammatical relations.

When we say that these languages have a monosyllabic basis, we do not mean that they have no words of more than one syllable—as is the case in Chinese. But in the most typical examples of the family, we certainly find that the *greater number of the words, and especially the verbs, are monosyllables*, and that longer words are compounds, in which it is usually easy to make out the monosyllabic roots. Ellis says of Ewe: *

"All the words in the language are derived from the simple monosyllabic roots, consisting of a consonant followed by a vowel, each of which is in Ewe a verb. The same holds good for Tshi and Gã, and . . . these verbs . . . are probably the primitive roots of the language."

He goes on to give a list of them, to the number of 118. They are just like the syllables in a child's first reading book—*ba, be, bi, bo, bu,—da, de, di, do, du*, and so on, only that in Ewe, each of these syllables is a real word, with a meaning, and in English only a few of them happen to have any. Every possible combination of a consonant followed by a vowel is a word in Ewe, for even the few omitted (no doubt accidentally) from Ellis's list are to be found in Westermann's *Dictionary*.

But the number of such combinations being limited, it is obvious that there are not nearly enough to express all the ideas of a people in even the most rudimentary stage of culture—and the Ewe are far from being that. They have hit on the same expedient for multiplying sounds as the Chinese; the same syllable pronounced with a different pitch of the voice, is an entirely different word. Thus, **dà**,

* *The Ewe-speaking Peoples of the Slave Coast of West Africa*, p. 253.

with the low tone means "throw;" **dá**, with the high tone, "crawl"; **dó**, is "say"; **dò**, "be sad"; **do** (with the level intonation) "sleep." Even so, there are often several different meanings for the same sound, but probably no great difficulty arises for a practised speaker. We must remember how seldom any one but a foreigner imperfectly acquainted with English gets confused by the different senses of such words as "page," "can," "bay," or between "sea" and "see," "be" and "bee," etc. It is obvious that, in learning such a language it is all-important to pay sufficient attention to the tones, and the same may, to a certain extent, be said of the Bantu languages.

In *Nuba* "the majority of the verbs are of one syllable, likewise some of the nouns. Reinisch says: 'Most verb-roots are monosyllabic. Verb-stems consisting of two or more syllables are compounds, and in most cases the component parts can be easily recognised'" (Westermann).

The same is the case in Dinka, though here the verbs (unlike Nuba, where the roots are made up of one consonant and one vowel) consist of consonant + vowel + consonant, as **bog**, "throw," **bur**, "fish," etc.

But in general, in these eastern languages, the monosyllabic character is less clear than in the western. This is only what might be expected, since they have been far more in contact with alien influences.

When we analyse words of more than one syllable, we often find that they consist of independent, unaltered words placed side by side. Thus, in Ewe, **dzena** (it might equally well be written **dze na**, just as we write "throw back," "put away"), "bear fruit," is composed of **dze**, "sprout," and **na**, "give," and **dome**, "enter," of **do**, "go," and **me**, "inside." How little these component elements are really amalgamated, appears from the fact that there is no accented syllable, but each syllable has the same stress. Of course, in a strictly monosyllabic language, the stress-accent is an impossibility; and, though the pitch-accent is not impossible in an agglutinating or inflected language (the two kinds coexist in Bantu) it is seldom of equal importance with the other.

In Ibo, too, most simple verbs are of one syllable; those of two are clearly compounds, as **buda,** "bring down," from **bu,** "carry," and **da,** "fall," or **kpagbu,** "throttle," from **kpa,** "squeeze," and **gbu,** "kill."

Sometimes we find that nouns are derived from verbs by prefixing a vowel (usually *a*) or a nasal (*m* or *n*). Thus, in Tshi we have, from **wu,** "to die," **awu,** "murder," and **owu,** "death"; in Yoruba **bo,** "to worship," **abo,** "worshipper" and so on.

The meaning of this prefix is not certain, but it seems probable that it was originally a demonstrative pronoun which has either lost its meaning or changed its form. If so, such compounds are a step away from the purely isolating stage in language. But in any case this prefix is not an inflexion in the sense of marking the *grammatical relations* of a word (number, gender, tense, case, etc.): it is on a par with such suffixes as *-ness*, which makes a noun out of an adjective, *-ly*, which is used in the formation of adverbs, etc. *Grammatical relations* exist to a certain extent in Sudanian speech, though they are not marked by inflexions.

Gender.—There is, as we have already said, no *gender*. This does not mean that the speakers of Sudanian languages take no account of sex-distinction, but that they *do not express it by any change in the shape of a word.* There is not even a separate feminine pronoun, and African natives who learn English find it difficult at first to understand the use of "he" and "she," or to see why they should not say "sir" to a lady. A good illustration is the classic instance of Winwood Reade's interpreter, who not knowing the word for "daughter," asked, "What you say when him son be girl?" and consistently called the daughter "him" after the explanation had been given.

When it is necessary to express the distinction, it is sometimes done by using different words—as if they were considering two beings of different species, not two of the same species with a difference. Thus we have in Ewe—

	Tó = father.	**Nò** = mother.
	Fò = elder brother.	**Dǎ** = elder sister.
In Gã:	**Nu** = man.	**Yo** = woman.
	Wu = husband.	**Nã** = wife.
In Kunama:	**Buta** = male.	**Shina** = female (of animals).
In Nuba:	**Id** = man.	**Eny** = woman.*

Or else, the words for "male" and "female" are placed before or after the words to be distinguished, just as we say "he-goat," "she-goat," etc.

Gã: **china-nu,** "bull"; **china-yo,** "cow." †

Sometimes the same word is used without distinction, as in Kunama—

Afo, "grandparent"; **imbo,** "uncle," "aunt"; **isha,** "younger brother," "younger sister."

In addition to the above ways of indicating a feminine, Tshi sometimes adds **a** to a masculine word, which when the word already ends in **a** means lengthening the final vowel—as **ata** "twin brother," **atã** "twin sister." This **a** is really a contraction of **wa,** "child," and therefore stands on the same level with the last mentioned procedure; but it is interesting, because it shows (a point to which we shall return in Chapter VI.) that originally the sex distinction coincided with that between large and small

* In Meinhof's alphabet **eń**, in Phonetic script **eɲ**: the sound of the **ny** is like the French **gn** in **digne.**

† **China** (like Tshi **nantwi,** Bantu **ng'ombe, inkomo,** etc.), a neutral word, corresponding to our *neat* (Scots *nowt*), German *Rind*; so that **china-nu** is literally "man-neat," **china-yo** "woman-neat."

objects. Shilluk has something like a rudimentary indication of gender, in the case of two words only, and perhaps there is something of the same kind in Lang'o. These, with Acholi (Gang), Lur and Dho-Luo ("Nilotic Kavirondo" or Nyifwa) may perhaps be grouped together as a "Nilotic" subdivision of the Sudan family.

Number.—Sometimes there is really no indication of the plural, as in Ibo. Mr. F. W. H. Migeod says* that when he was trying to obtain the plural forms of words in West African languages, "uneducated natives . . . were quite unable to express this relation, unless the word were incorporated in a sentence. Even then, they usually made considerable difficulty over it and invariably wanted to indicate a definite number or *many*. . . . Languages can be found that furnish examples of every step or stage in the evolution of the plural form. The first and lowest stage is that in which the idea of a grammatical plural is absolutely non-existent. The noun remains unchanged. It is in its primitive state of being the name of a thing. Such . . . language only recognises a proper name or noun, not a common noun; and, as in English, the name of a person or place cannot, except in a distorted way, take a plural form, so the name of a thing in such a language can also receive no change. In order to represent what is understood by plurality, either the word must be repeated, or a word expressing number or quantity joined with it. In Ibo, for instance, if a numeral adjective be not added to the noun, the word **ntutu** ("many") precedes it. Very frequently, though, the context of a sentence supplies all that is necessary. Even in other languages, in which there is a regular plural inflexion, it is a common practice to use the noun in the singular—that is, without change—if accompanied by a numeral or other adjective expressing quantity. . . . The next stage is the amalgamation of

* *The Languages of West Africa*, vol. i. pp. 162, 163.

some such word as 'people,' 'many,' 'they,' with the noun itself."

Thus, in Ewe, **wo**, "they," is added to a noun in the singular:

Ka = "string," **ka-wo** = "strings";
ati = "tree," plural, **ati-wo**.

In Tshi, they add **nom** "people," or **fo** "person" (a singular with a collective force), or indicate the plural by a change of prefix.

Aga, "father"; plural, **aga-nom.**
Afe, "companion"; plural, **afe-fo.**
Ohene, "king"; plural, **ahene.**

In Yoruba, the pronoun **awo** ("they") is prefixed to indicate the plural, or sometimes the noun is reduplicated. No plural sign is considered necessary if the noun is accompanied by a numeral. Ellis says, "The plural is formed by placing the demonstrative **wonyi** (these) or **wonni** (those) after the noun, except when a number is used." This may refer to a different dialect from that where **awo** is used. But it is quite possible that both forms exist side by side.

It may be asked how, if there is no inflexion to indicate the plural, there can be singular and plural pronouns. The answer is that, just as there are separate, unrelated words to indicate "male" and "female," there are also different words for "he" (or "it") and "they." The reason, Mr. Migeod suggests, is "the negro's conception of a thing having an independent individuality," or, in other words, it never occurs to him that "they" is a modification of "he";—it is something which makes quite a distinct impression on his mind, and requires a separate word to express it. To children, as their perceptions gradually awaken, each fresh person or thing which comes within their ken is the only one of its kind, and the only names they know are proper names. There is one person called Dada, one called Nana, one dog (name as the case may be); and it takes a good deal of experience to show them that there exist others like them. Still later comes the realization of *species* and *genera*: "fathers," "nurses," "dogs," "men," "women," "animals"; but this is necessary (at least in some rudimentary degree) before the mind can grasp such an apparently simple conception as that of *plurality*, "more-than-one-ness."

The conception of mere *number* is an abstract one at which the primitive mind arrives comparatively late. And the idea of number in general is more abstract than that of particular numbers: one, two, three. M. Lévy-Bruhl,* suggests that the reason why people on the level, say, of the Klamath Indians, have no plural in their language, is "that this form is not sufficiently explicit; it does not specify ... whether the subjects or objects are two, or three, or few, or many; whether they are together or separate. Such languages have no general terms, *e.g.*, for 'tree' or 'fish,' though they have names for every kind of either. They will, therefore, be able to express —not the idea of plurality in general, but different kinds of plurals."

Dinka exhibits an interesting phenomenon, which we must notice before passing on to relations of *case*. Besides the plural formed by suffixing **-ke** (the pronoun equivalent to "they" or "these"; as in **dyonkor-ke**, "horses") there is another, formed by *changing the quantity of the vowel:* if it is short in the singular it becomes long in the plural, and *vice versâ*. Thus, **rŏr**, "forest," becomes in the plural **rōr**, and **răl**, "vein," **rāl**. This may be connected with the *Law of Polarity*, which we shall have to discuss when we come to the Hamitic Languages.

* *Les Fonctions Mentales dans les Sociétés Inférieures* (Paris, 1910), p. 155.

Dinka, as has already been remarked, has, like Kunama, probably been influenced by the speech of neighbouring, non-Sudanian tribes.

Case.—There is no difference of form between the subject and object of the verb; the only way to tell which is which is by position. The order of the sentence is—

	Subject	Verb	Direct Object.
Thus:	**e**	**kpo**	**fla**
	"He	saw	(the) king" (Ewe).
	O	**sũ**	**ne nua**
	"He	mourns	his brother" (Tshi).

The Indirect Object, if there is one, may be placed after the direct object, as—

e na ga fofo
"He gave money (to his) father" (Ewe).

But it is more usual to take the indirect object out of the sentence altogether and give it a verb to itself—

e di ga na fofo
"He sought money gave father."

i.e., "He sought money for his father."

The position of the direct object is the same as in Bantu,* after the verb, but the position of a noun in the possessive is the reverse: *the genitive precedes its governing noun.* The Gold Coast native says, "the man's house"; the Zulu or Muganda, "the house of the man."

Professor Meinhof explains this by saying that to the Negro the possessor is the most important thing, whereas the Bantu (and also the Hamite) argues—unconsciously, no doubt—that there must be a house before any one can have it. The possessive is usually expressed by

* *I.e.*, when the object is a *noun*, the **Bantu** object-pronoun immediately precedes the verb, as we shall see in the next chapter.

simple juxtaposition: one word following the otner without any connecting particle.

Ohene mmra = "the king (his) law" (Tshi).
Ila masa = "Ila's lance" (Kunama).

Sometimes the two words are connected by an invariable particle equivalent to "his," "her," or "their"—

fofo fe ale
"father his sheep" (Ewe).

obofo ne nua
"messenger his brother" (Tshi).

ash in gida
"year its pastness" (Kunama) = "last year."

ile ti baba
"house of father" (Yoruba).

Yoruba and Efik (like Dinka and some other languages in the same area) are exceptions to the rule, probably, as Westermann points out, through contact with Hamitic speech, since "both Hausas and Fulbe * have for a long time past lived among the Yorubas and influenced their social and political life"—in fact the Yoruba language contains various Hausa expressions.

Tenses.—The verb undergoes no changes in conjugation, either in the singular or plural. Differences of tense are marked by auxiliary verbs. Thus, in Ewe, the simple present tense of **wo**, "do," is **me wo** = "I do," **e wo** = "he does," etc.; a habitual tense is formed by adding **na**, "stay"; **me wo na** = "I do stay" "I stay doing," *i.e.*, "I am in the habit of doing." In the same way, **vo** = "finish" is used to make the perfect and **va** = "come" for the future.

One of the most striking peculiarities to be noticed in

* The people usually called "Fulas" or "Fulani." The peculiar form Fulbe will be explained in Chapter VI.

these languages is the absence of prepositions and the way in which their work is done by verbs and nouns. It seems as though we could watch the process by which this part of speech arose; it is a late development and does not exist, *e.g.*, in Chinese.

A native of Togo, if he wants to express, "I am going to the town," says, "I go, reach town's inside," or, for "he went to Lome," "he went, reached Lome," in Ewe, **e yi de Lome.** So also—

E tso ati foe "He took stick hit him" (Ewe); *i.e.*, "he hit him with a stick." "Inside the house" is "house('s) inside." "He jumped from the ship into the sea" is "He jumped, left ship's inside, fell sea's inside." "Up," "down," "before," "behind," are "top," "bottom," "face," "back." We use these nouns similarly in English, though we cannot get on without connecting prepositions; "at the back of," "on the top of," etc. This is also to some extent the case in Bantu. In Zulu, we have the adverbs, **pezulu,** "above" (literally **pa-izulu,** "on the sky"), **pa-nsi,** "below" (literally "on the ground").* These are quite recognizable; but **ndani,** the Swahili for "within," is the locative for an entirely obsolete word, still used in some of the inland languages, **nda,** "stomach."

Some curious examples of this kind of construction are found in Dinka—

ping tar, "earth's bottom" = underground.
mul kou, "donkey's back" = on a donkey.
yut nom, "house's head" = on, or over the house.
keror te, "snake's place" = instead of the snake.

So, too, in Shilluk, "the prepositions are nouns and are treated as such" (Westermann).

* In Karanga (Mashonaland), "on account of," "for the sake of," are rendered by "on the back of." The literal rendering of a sentence meaning "the tribes for whose sake we went to Africa" is "those tribes we went to Africa on their back!"

There are likewise no conjunctions, and therefore, no conditional or dependent sentences, as a rule, though Mende (Sierra Leone) has a remarkable way of rendering "if," viz., **ina,** which is **i** = "it," **na** = "there," *i.e.*, "put that there" and see what is the result!

Before passing from this subject, I must direct attention to a large class of words, which have an important bearing on the history of speech. They have been noticed in various Bantu languages, and probably exist in all; but, as Westermann has recently pointed out, they also constitute a remarkable feature in Ewe, and close inquiry would, no doubt, reveal them elsewhere, where they have not yet been noticed. German writers call them "sound-pictures" (*Lautbilder*) or "word-pictures" (*Wortbilder*); they have also been designated "*onomatopoeias*" and "descriptive adverbs." Perhaps "interjectional roots" describes them as well as any other term. They are invariable words, imitating, or at least expressing, not merely sounds and movements, but (in a way difficult if not impossible to explain in any European language) form, position and even colour, taste and smell. Ewe is extraordinarily rich in them; they are functionally adverbs since they qualify the action signified by a verb, but some may be classed as adjectives. But they only apply to one particular action, state or quality, and are, therefore, always used with one special verb or noun and never found in any other connection. Westermann gives thirty-three such *Lautbilder* used with the one verb, **zo,** "to walk," and says, that these by no means exhaust the list. A few may be quoted as specimens.

Zo ka ka, "to walk upright."

Zo dze dze, "an assured and energetic gait."

Zo tya tya, "to walk quickly."

Zo si si, "said of small people, lightly stepping along."

Zo boho boho, "the heavy walk of a stout man."

Zo tyo tyo, "the firm and deliberate gait of a tall person."

Zo kpudu kpudu, "the quick, hurried gait of a small man."

Zo wudo wudo, "a quiet, graceful way of walking," said chiefly of women.

Zo gowu gowu, "to walk with a slight limp, the head leaning forward."

Zo lumo lumo, "running of small animals, such as rats and mice."

There are many other words of this kind, which describe the various actions of running, crawling, swimming, riding, etc., etc., but the above are quite enough to illustrate the point.

It is certain that real words, capable of inflexion, such as substantives, verbs and adjectives, have originated in such words as these. Westermann gives numerous examples. In this connection, it is interesting to refer to the late Dean Farrar's *Language and Languages*—a book which, though in some respects obsolete, contains a great deal of interesting and suggestive matter. (See especially the Chapters on "Interjections" and "*Lautgeberden* or Vocal Gestures," pp. 75-93.) His views on "onomatopoeias" have received a striking confirmation from the results of African research.

We may remark, in passing, that true adjectives are rare in these—as they are in the Bantu languages. They are often, as we shall see in the next chapter, expressed by verbs.

It will not have escaped the reader that some of the *Lautbilder* quoted above consist of two syllables. I am not aware at present that any one has mentioned this as a difficulty; and I do not feel that I know enough about this language-family to advance any theory in explanation. But it is not inconceivable that the monosyllabic character of Sudan speech may not be original but acquired—as is now known to be the case in Chinese; * words have been worn down from two or more syllables to one by loss of medial consonants and contraction of vowels, and in other ways, just as in French, *cage* comes from the Latin *cavea*, *rage* from *rabie(m)*, *eau* from *aqua* and so forth. One thing seems clear—original roots are not *necessarily* monosyllables.

Though the true character of these languages has only been ascertained within the last few years, they have been separately studied for a much longer period. The oldest attempt is perhaps a Fetu † vocabulary published in 1673 by a Danish pastor named Müller. Since then a number of dictionaries, grammars and translations have been produced by missionaries and others, many of them (the Basel Mission being among the oldest established in West Africa), German and Swiss. The whole Bible has been translated ịnto Tshi, Gã, Yoruba, and Efik, besides partial translations into a good many other languages.

Our examples and illustrations have chiefly been taken from the languages of the Gold Coast and Lower Niger, because these are the best known, and, on the whole, the most typical; but there are others, far too numerous to mention, some of which are at least equally interesting. There is the very wide-spread Mande or Mandingo, spoken in Senegambia, and French Guinea, and part of Sierra Leone; the Vai (Liberia), remarkable for possessing a written character invented in or about 1834 by Doalu Bukere; Bulom and Temne, in the Sierra Leone Protectorate, which, by some, have been placed in the Bantu family; Songhai, on the bend of the Middle Niger; Jukum and Munshi, in the little known region of the Benue—these are only a few of the most important.

* See extracts quoted in *Descriptive Sociology*, No. IX., Div. III. *Chinese*, by E. T. C. Werner (1910), p. 231.

† The Fetu tribe, now merged in the Fanti, occupied the country in the neighbourhood of Elmina. Their language is practically identical with Fanti.

Equally impossible is it to notice the books that have been written on these languages—a list of those most likely to be useful is given in the Appendix. French officials both civil and military, have done excellent work in this direction, as well as English and German missionaries. I need only mention the names of the late General Faidherbe and of Monsieur Maurice Delafosse.

One point of interest, however, must not be forgotten We owe the standard grammars of Yoruba and Nupe (at least I am not aware that they have been superseded), a number of vocabularies and a mass of valuable miscellaneous information, to the late Bishop Crowther, a native of Yoruba, originally named Adjai. His son, and other native clergy have also done valuable linguistic work, and it is gratifying to find that several Yorubas have written (in English) interesting accounts of their people's customs and beliefs.*

The principal languages belonging to the Sudanian family (including all those mentioned in this chapter) are marked on the map at the end of the book.

TEXTS.

SHILLUK.†

Áfóájo̱	**é**	**wè̱lò̱**	**kí̱**	**Jwó̱k,**	**è**	**bȅ̱dò̱**	**kí̱**	**ṱá**
Hare	he	travels	with	Jwok,	he	stays	in	under

yâṱ.	**Jwó̱k**	**é**	**nȅ̱nò̱**	**ká**	**áfȯájò̱**	**é**	**bȅ̱dò̱**
tree.	Jwok	he	sleeps	and	hare	he	stays

* See R. E. Dennett, *At the Back of the Black Man's Mind* (Appendix), and *Nigerian Studies* (Preface).

† From Westermann, *The Shilluk People, their Language and Folk-lore* (Philadelphia, 1912). In Westermann's text ´ indicates the high, ` the low, - the level tone, ^ the falling, ˇ the rising.

The tones are not marked in the I.P.A. transcript, but the Association suggests the following notation: high level, ē; low level, e̱; mid level unmarked; falling, è; rising, é.

mál. Kā jē bê̱no̱, ge̱ gīr, afoajo̱ ko:
upright. And people come, they many, hare said:
Dwòṭí mâl, léń á bi. Jwó̱k è kò kí̱né: Bē̱di
Rise up, war has come. Jwok he says thus: Stay
yau. Ká léń é bê̱nò̱, kámá mak afoajo̱ ki
just. And war it comes, begins (to) seize hare and
Jwó̱k. Jwò̱k è ko: Afoajo̱ mak tyàlá, ká tyàle̱
Jwok. Jwok he says: Hare, seize feet-my and feet-his
mâk, ká Jwó̱k é wā́ńò̱. Ká léń é ké̱ḓò
(he) seized and Jwok he disappears. And war it goes,
ká Jwó̱k è ko: Afoajo̱, ké̱ṯ! *
and Jwok he says: Hare, go!

The Same in I.P.A. Script.

ɑfoɑɟɔ e wɛlɔ kɪ ɟwɔk e bɛːdɔ kɪ ta jɑt. ɟwɔk e nɛːnɔ kɑ ɑfoɑɟɔ e bɛːḍɔ mɑl. kɑː ɟeː bɛːnɔ, gɛ gɪːr ɑfoɑɟɔ koː dwoti mɑl, leɲ ɑ bi. ɟwɔk e ko kɪne: bɛːḍi jɑu. kɑ leɲ e bɛɪnɔ, kɑmɑ mɑk ɑfoɑɟɔ kɪ ɟwɔk. ɟwɔk e koː ɑfoɑɟɔ mɑk cɑlɑ, kɑ cɑle mɑk, kɑ ɟwɔk e wɑɪnɔ. kɑ leɲ e kɛdɔ kɑ ɟwɔk e koː ɑfoɑɟɔ, kɛt! †

Free Translation.

One day, the hare and Jwok (a spirit) went on a journey together. They stopped under a tree; Jwok went to sleep,

* It appears that the tones in Shilluk sometimes change, according to laws not yet fully ascertained. In general, says Westermann, a word, when pronounced by itself, "has its fixed tone," but in connection with other words the intonation changes very strongly, adapting itself to" or distinguishing itself from the adjacent words. In the above extract the word *afoajo̱* has one set of tones where it begins a sentence and another where it comes in the middle of one, as in the second line. The tone is not marked on this word where it occurs in the third, fifth, sixth and eighth lines.

† In this script, t, d, and n, when left unmarked, have the dental pronunciation; a dot under the letter denotes that the sound is produced further back.

but the Hare stayed awake. A great many people came along, and the Hare awakened Jwok, saying, "Rise up, the enemy has come." Jwok said, "Never mind, just stay here." The enemy came and were just going to seize them, when Jwok said, "Hare, take hold of my feet!" The Hare did so, and Jwok disappeared. The enemy passed on (and left them), and Jwok said, "Hare, go!"

B. Luke xv. 11–14.

Jal mēko̱ wa̱t áryàu ; a kōbi̱ ńa ńal ṱēṋ ki̱ne : wuo,
Man some son two ; said child boy small thus : father,
ṱōṱe yan ki̱ bun a mea kí̱ rē jam. A fā̱ni
give me with part which mine with goods. He divided
jámé̱ kí̱ gé̱n. Ka rũmi̱ chaṅ maṅô̱k ńa ńal ṱēṋ
goods-his with them. And finished days few child boy small
á chò̱ñà jámé ka wé̱lí fōṱe málá̱wí̱ ; ki̱
he gathered goods-his and travelled country far ; with
kā́ é̱ní a wé̱tí̱ jámé̱ kí̱ ré̱ chám. Ká rũmí̱
place this he squandered his-goods with eating. And finished
ki̱ wè̱té jâm, ka ke̱ch e bê̱nò̱, ka
with squandering goods and hunger he came, and
wíjé̱ mûm.
head-his perplexed.

The Same in I.P.A. Script.

ɟal mɛ:kɔ wʌṭ * arjʌu; a ko:bɪ ɲa ɲal te:n kɪṇe; wuo,
to:te jaṇ kɪ buṇ a mea kɪ re: ɟam. a fʌ:ṇɪ ɟamɛ kɪ geṇ.
ka ru:mɪ tʃaŋ maɲɔk ɲa ɲal te:n a tʃɔŋa ɟamɛ ka wɛ:li
fo:te malʌwɪ; kɪ ka: ɛṇi a wɛṭɪ ɟamɛ kɪ re: tʃam. ka
ru: mɪ kɪ wɛte ɟam, ka kɛtʃ e bɛ:ṇɔ, ka wiɟɛ mum.

* ʌ represents the "indeterminate vowel"—the sound of *u* in "*but*."

2. GÃ (AKRA).

Gbo̱bilo̱ ke̱ e̱-ṅã.
(The) hunter and his wife.

[From Zimmermann's *Grammatical Sketch of the Akra or Gã Language* (1858).]

Mi-tã lō mi-tã-a ? [1]
I mention or I mention not ?

Wo̱ miṅ here no̱ !
We are-receiving it ! (*i.e.* " we are listening ").

Dže̋ nū ko ke̱ e-ṅā ní [2] **ame̱-yo̱.**
There-was man (a) certain and his wife who they lived.

Ni a-tšeo̱ e-ṅã gbe̱i, ake̱ : [3] **Badŭa. Ni**
And she is called his wife, name, that is : Badua. And

ame̱-yo kose̱, ni nū le̱ gbo̱bio̱ ; [4] **ni lo hõmõ**
they lived bush, and man this hunted, and fish scarcity

baba, ní [2] **a-na-a mle̱ tete a fã**
came, which they got not mushrooms even they root-up

ni aho po ; ši Badua le̱ e-wu le̱ ke̱
and they cook even ; but Badua this, her husband this if

e-te gbo̱bimo, e-naä [5] **lo kẽ e-gbeo̱** [6] **ke̱ba.**
he went hunting, he gets fish still, he kills, he brings.

Ši agbe̱ne̱ le nū le̱ e-na-a lo le̱ eko e-gbe doṅ [7]
But now man this he got not fish this any to kill again.

[Notes 1 to 7 will be found on p. 54.]

CONNECTED TRANSLATION.

Once upon a time there lived a man and his wife, and the wife's name was Badua. They lived in the bush, and the husband used to hunt (*i.e.* fish) ; and there came a time of great scarcity, people could not even find mushrooms to cook. Now Badua's husband, when he went hunting, used to get fish and kill it and bring it home, but now he could no longer get any fish at all.

NOTES.

[1] *-a* is suffixed to the verb to denote the negative. The question (= "Shall I tell the story ?") and answer are the regular preliminary to a tale.

[2] *Ní* "who," "which," has the high tone, *ni* "and," the level.

[3] *Ake*, literally "they say," "people say," here has the force of "that is to say," "namely," or some such expression. The Bantu verb *ti* "say" is similarly used.

[4] "Hunting" would seem to include fishing, unless the word printed *lo* ("fish") in our text should have been *lō* "meat."

[5] *Enaä*, thus written, is affirmative, to be distinguished from the negative *enaa*, which occurs in the next line. In the first case the two vowels are sounded separately, in the second they are merely heard as a long *a*.

[6] The suffix *-o* indicates habitual action.

[7] This word, when pronounced by a native has the final *n* prolonged so as to suggest a doubling of the consonant. This effect, however, is really due to the rising intonation, which should also be noticed in the final vowel of *dže*. No attempt has here been made (with one exception) to mark the tones, but if the above extract is read aloud by a native, they will be heard in every word.

The sound written *gb* (or, in its voiceless form *kp*) is very characteristic of the Sudan languages. It is called by Meinhof "labio-velar" and is pronounced by placing the tongue in position to say *g* (or *k*) and then saying *b* (or *p*). No symbol has as yet been assigned to it by the International Phonetic Association. The extract, in I.P.A. script, runs as follows :—

gbɔ:bilɔ kɛ ɛŋɑ̃

mitɑ̃ lo: mitɑ̃ɑ̃?

wɔ min here nɔ.

dʒe: nu: ko kɛ eŋɑ̃ ni ɑmɛjɔ. ni ɑtʃɛɔ eŋɑ̃ gbɛi ɑkɛ badua. ni ɑmɛjɔ kosɛ, ni nu: lɛ gbɔbiɔ; ni lo hõmõ baba, ni ɑnɑ: mlɛ tete ɑ fɑ̃ ni ɑho po; ʃi badua lɛ, ewu lɛ kɛ ete gbɔbimo, enɑɑ lo kẽ egbeɔ kɛba. ʃi ɑgbɛnɛ lɛ nu: lɛ enɑ: lo lɛ eko egbe doŋ.

CHAPTER IV.

THE BANTU FAMILY.

The phonology of the Bantu languages does not come within the scope of this book, but we may say, generally, that with few exceptions, they contain no very strange or difficult sounds. The clicks found in Zulu and the cognate dialects of Cape Colony were adopted from Hottentots or Bushmen. (They will be referred to again in Chapter VII.) The "laterals" (usually written hl, dhl, tl, tlh) are also peculiar to the southern group of languages, and there are a few other sounds of limited range which need not be discussed here. In general the ordinary spelling—*i.e.*, that adopted by Steere for Swahili—will be sufficient to represent the examples given in this chapter.

Bantu words are almost invariably accented on the penultimate syllable. So rigidly is this law applied in most cases that, when an extra syllable is suffixed to a word, the stress is shifted forward, *e.g.*, in Swahili, **nyúmba** = a "house," when it takes **-ni** for the locative, becomes **nyumbáni**= "in the house." *

* Luganda, Konde (North Nyasa) and some others appear to accent the *root* syllable, without shifting the stress, when the position of that syllable is changed by the addition of suffixes. The truth seems to be that there are two kinds of stress, the *etymological*, on the root-syllable, and the *rhythmic*, which is usually on the penultimate, but occasionally on the ante-penultimate. The latter is, in the majority of Bantu languages, by far the most noticeable, so that the statement in the text may be taken as a broad, *general* rule. Details belong to the fuller study of each separate language.

Intonation is found side by side with stress,* and is very important in some languages (*e.g.*, Shambala) though apparently quite absent from others (*e.g.*, Swahili).

Syllables are always *open*. The apparent exceptions can usually be explained, by the dropping of a vowel; *e.g.*, the Xosa possessive pronouns **wam**, **bam**, etc., are really shortened from **wami**, **bami**, the forms still used in Zulu. The Chwana locative termination **ng** (as in Mafeking) corresponds with the Zulu locative **-ni** (of Tekwini, the Zulu name for Durban—literally " at the Bay "), and so has probably dropped a vowel; but, in any case, the accent does not fall on the final syllable, as the **ng** makes a syllable by itself. (Pronounce MA-FE-KÍ-NG; this is not difficult if we remember the way the words " king," " sing " are sometimes divided in singing).

As already mentioned, the first peculiarity that strikes a European on making acquaintance with any Bantu language is the *system of prefixes*. Or rather, if he has no knowledge of this system to guide him, he will be bewildered by the number of forms under which the simplest words present themselves to him. He cannot learn the equivalents for " two," " three," " my," " your," " his," without knowing of *whom* or *what* there are two or three, *what* is possessed by me or you. Take Swahili: " two

* This fact cannot be too much insisted on. It has been entirely overlooked in many otherwise competent grammars; while others give the merest hint of it. Thus in Brown's *Secwana Dictionary*, we read (p. 6): " In some cases only a very slight difference in sound or emphasis " (really *pitch* or *intonation*) " distinguishes one word from another. . . . Fortunately, such words are not numerous." The Rev. A. J. Wookey (*Secwana Grammar*, p. 9) takes a juster view of the matter, though he, too, uses the word " accentuation " for " pitch." Mr. D. Jones is of opinion that there are at least four distinct tones in this language, and that " to ignore [them] in speaking, must be quite as bad, if not worse, than speaking English without making any difference between the vowels in *bed, bad, bud, bird.*" Cf. also *Elements of Luganda Grammar* (S.P.C.K., 1903), p. 144.

people" is **watu wawili,** "two trees" **miti miwili,** "two knives" **visu viwili,** "my child" **mtoto wangu,** "my name" **jina langu,** "my house," **nyumba yangu,** "my houses" **nyumba zangu.** Once the principle is known the seeming confusion becomes clear. If we may be allowed to quote again from Brother Hyacinth, the Capuchin missionary, "the language of the Congos and others of Negro lands, is not founded nor forms its rules upon the declension of words, but on their principiation . . . and varied accordingly."

It was explained in Chapter II. that the prefix of any given class (or "principiation") of nouns (corresponding, roughly, to a declension in Latin or Greek) reappears in connection with every adjective, verb or pronoun agreeing with the noun, and that this system is known as the *Alliterative Concord.*

The best way of illustrating this concord is by means of Bleek's classic sentences which, if somewhat nonsensical in themselves (as is the wont of grammatical examples), at least serve their purpose well enough. After explaining and analysing one of these, we shall give the list of original prefixes as drawn up by Bleek and completed by Meinhof, and follow it up with instances of the noun-classes as actually used in some of the best known Bantu languages.

Zulu is one of the most convenient languages to take illustrations from, because the prefixes being less worn down and altered than in some others, it is easier to see the concords. The following sentence exemplifies those of the first or person-class :—

Umu-ntu	**w-etu**	**omu-hle**	**u-ya-bonakala,**	**si-m-tanda.**
Man	our	handsome	he appears,	we love him.

Umuntu, properly speaking, is "person," as it may mean either "man" or "woman" according to circumstances;

where sex is indicated, different words are used. The root is **-ntu**, the prefix **umu**, which is in the plural exchanged for the prefix **aba**.

The **w-** of **wetu** is the **u** of this prefix, passing into **w** before a vowel; **-etu** is the root of the possessive pronoun for the first person plural.

-hle is the root of an adjective meaning "good," "fine," "handsome," etc.

Its prefix is **omu**—not **umu**—because the relative particle **a**, originally prefixed to it, has coalesced with the *u*. (In Zulu, whenever *u* follows *a*, they usually run together and form the broad sound of *o*, like *ou* in ought.) So that **umuntu omuhle** is really "the man who is handsome." When the adjective is used *predicatively* (that is in such a sentence as "the man is handsome") the prefix drops its initial vowel: **umu-ntu muhle.**

U- is the form which the prefix assumes when used with the verb; in other words, it is the pronoun representing nouns of the person-class; it is also used as the pronoun of the third person singular (corresponding to either "he" or "she") when it is implied that the subject of the verb is of the person-class, though no noun is expressed. But, though **u-ya-bonakala** may stand alone, meaning "he appears," the *u* must never be omitted when the noun is present. With us, it is unnecessary repetition to say "the man *he* appears": in Bantu, we should never find "the man appears" without a connecting particle in the shape of a first-class pronoun.

This pronoun, which in Zulu still exists in its primitive form *u*, has in Swahili and some other languages become changed to *a*. Into the reason for this change we cannot enter here.

Bonakala is the "neuter-passive form" of the verb **bona** = "see"; the "forms" of verbs will be discussed later. **Ya** is the sign of the "Emphatic" or "Continued"

Present—the one most commonly used in Zulu : **u-ya-bona** may be, but is not always, translated " he is seeing."

Si is the pronoun of the first person plural when prefixed to a verb. It cannot be used alone. " We " standing by itself is **tina**.

m, contracted for **mu,** is the object-pronoun for nouns of the first class, in the singular.

It will be seen that it is really the second syllable of the prefix, as the subject-pronoun is the first.

Tanda is a verb meaning " love " or " like."

In the plural this sentence will be—

Aba-ntu b-etu aba-hle ba-ya-bonakala, si-ba-tanda.
People our handsome they appear, we them love.

This needs no further explanation.

It will be interesting, as showing the state to which the prefixes have been reduced in some languages, to give the same sentence in Swahili :—

M-tu w-etu m-zuri a-na-onekana, tu-na-m-penda.

In the plural :—

Wa-tu- w-etu wa-zuri wa-na-onekana, tu-na-wa-penda.

Here most of the words are recognizable as the same, though there are different roots for " handsome " and " love." The form of the neuter-passive is somewhat different, but the root-verbs **bona** and **ona** are the same word. **Tu-** does not at first sight seem identical with **si-**, and may go back to a different root, but the Zulu separable pronoun is **tina**.

We usually reckon eight noun-classes in Zulu, but most languages have nine or ten. Bleek reckoned sixteen, treating the singulars and plurals as separate classes, and Meinhof has followed him, bringing the number up to 21, by counting the three forms of the locative as separate classes and adding three more, discovered since Bleek's time. For the present purpose it seems better to treat the singular and plural as one class ; and in this way, as there are some which have no plural, we get fifteen. The prefixes, according to Professor Meinhof (who thinks that the initial vowel, found *e.g.*, in Zulu, is a later addition) are in their original form as follows :—

I.	*Singular.*	*Plural.*
1.	**mu-**	**v̱a-***
2.	**mu-**	**mi-**
3.	**li-**	**ma-**
4.	**ki-**	**vî-**
5.	**ni-**	**lî-ni-**
6.	**lu-**	Same as 5, but occasionally **tu-**
7.	**ka-**	**tu-** occasionally **bu-**.
8.	**v̱u-**	No plural, as a rule.
9.	**ku-**	No plural.
10.	**pa**	Locatives. No plural.
11.	**ku**	
12.	**mu**	
13.	**pî-**	**tu-** (only found in Duala).
14.	**gu-**	**ga-**
15.	**gî-**	**gimi-**

* v̱ represents "bilabial v" (*v* pronounced with both lips, instead of, like our English *v*, with upper teeth and lower lip), which was according to Professor Meinhof the original pronunciation of this prefix. Some languages have made it into *ba*, some into *wa* or *a*, some, like Chwana ("Sechuana") keep the primitive sound. In the same way, the eighth prefix, *v̱u-* sometimes becomes *bu-* or *u-*. As *lu-* (sixth class) has also in many cases become *u-*, Classes 6 and 8 have sometimes been amalgamated—as in Swahili. The last two prefixes are written by Professor Meinhof with a Greek gamma representing the sound of the German *g* in *Sage*, a guttural which may be described as the voiced sound of Scots *ch* in "loch"—I.P.A. ɡ. For our present purpose it is more convenient to write these prefixes as they appear to be pronounced in the chief languages where (apparently) they still exist: Ganda and Gisu. The circumflex, which is important chiefly for etymological reasons, indicates the "heavy i," probably arising from the coalition of two vowels. It need not detain us at this stage, but is discussed in Meinhof, *Lautlehre*, p. 21.

[N.B.—In speaking of the languages treated of in this chapter, it has been found best to omit the prefix consistently all through and

Some of these only occur in a few languages; while, in some, there have been found traces of additional classes, not given here, so that we may fairly conclude the whole number to have been formerly greater than it is now. There will be something to say on this head in the sixth chapter.

The examples illustrating the different classes are taken from Zulu and Swahili, except in cases where a class does not exist in either of those two languages and has to be supplied from elsewhere. Appended to each noun is a numeral in agreement with it ("one" in the singular, "two" in the plural) and the possessive particle (equivalent to "of"), which does not occur in the sentence already given.

	Singular.	*Plural.*
Class I.		
Zulu.*	**Um-ntwana mu-nye wa.**	**Aba-ntwana aba-bili ba.**
Swahili.	**M-toto m-moja wa.**	**Wa-toto wa-wili wa.**
	One child of.	Two children of.
Class II.		
Zulu.	**Umu-ti** (tree) **mu-nye wa.**	**Imi-ti emi-bili ya.**
Swahili.	**M-ti m-moja wa.**	**Mi-ti mi-wili ya.**
Class III.		
Zulu.	**I(li) -zinyo** (tooth) **li-nye la.**	**Ama-zinyo ama-bili a.**
Swahili.†	**Jino moja la.**	**M-eno ma-wili ya.**

say Ganda (not Luganda), Sutu (not Sesutu), Chwana, Nyanja, etc., as well as Swahili, Yao, Zulu. The spelling Kongo is used for the language to which the name more particularly belongs (namely that of the Lower River and the Saõ Salvador country, of which we have a splendid Dictionary, the work of the late Rev. W. Holman Bentley), and Congo for the river, and, in a general way for the whole region and its inhabitants.]

* The numeral "one" in Zulu never has the initial vowel. **Omunye** means "other."

† This class, in Swahili, loses its prefix altogether, except when ple given the initial consonant of the stem (represented in Zulu by **z** is dropped in the plural): **meno** is for **ma-ino**.

	Singular.	*Plural.*
Class IV.		
Zulu.	**Isi-hlalo** * (chair) **si-nye sa.**	**Izi-hlalo ezi-bili za.**
Swahili.	**Ki-ti ki-moja cha.**	**Vi-ti vi-wili vya.**
Class V.		
Zulu.	**I-ndhlu** (house) **inye ya.**	**Izi-ndhlu ezi-mbili za.**
Swahili.	**Nyumba moja ya.**	**Nyumba mbili za.**
Class VI.		
Zulu.	**U(lu)-ti** (stick) **lu-nye lwa.**	**Izi-nti ezi-mbili za.**
Swahili.†	**U-ti umoja wa.**	**Nyuti mbili za.**
Class VII.		
Ganda.‡	**Aka-ti** (little stick) **aka-mu ka.**	**Obu-ti obu-biri bwa.**
Class VIII.		
Zulu.	**Ubu-suku (night) bunye ba.**	No plural.
Swahili.	**U-siku umoja (or mmoja) wa.**	**ma-siku.** §
Class IX.		
Zulu.	**Uku-fa** (death) **kunye kwa.**	No plural.
Swahili.	**Ku-fa kumoja kwa.**	No plural.
Class X.‖		
Nyanja.	**Pa nyumba pamodzi pa** = "at the one house of" . . .	

* From **hlala,** "to sit" —see below, p. 70. **Ki-ti** is from the same root as **m-ti** (also **u-ti** and **aka-ti,** below)—the primitive seat is a block of wood, and most African tribes use stools cut out of a solid tree-trunk.

† The sixth and eighth classes have coalesced in Swahili (**ulu** and **ubu** being both contracted into **u**) and have their concords like the second. Some nouns have lost their prefixes altogether and gone into the third.

‡ This "diminutive" class has disappeared from a good many languages and, in Ganda, has changed its plural prefix. It exists in Nyanja, but again with a different plural prefix **ti** :—**ka-ntu** "a little thing," plural **ti-ntu. Otu-** exists in Ganda as the prefix of a different class, meaning "a small quantity of anything," *e.g.* **Otu-dzi** "a drop of water."

§ Also **siku**, which would seem to have arisen through confusion with Class VI. Nouns of the eighth class, in some languages (as Herero and Chwana), when they can take a plural at all, take **ma-**.

‖ This class exists in Swahili, but as the locative in **-ni** has taken the place of the prepositions **pa, ku, mu**, it has no prefix. We say **nyumbani pa** for "at the house of," **nyumbani kwa** for "to the house of" (this **kw** must be distinguished from that of Class IX.—the concords are the same, though the meaning is not), **nyumbani mwa,** "in the house of."

	Singular.	*Plural.*
Class XI.		
Nyanja.	**Ku nyumba kumodzi kwa** = "to the one house of" . . .	
Class XII.		
Nyanja.	**Mu nyumba mmodzi mwa** = "in the one house of" . . .	
Class XIII.		
Duala.	**I-seru** (a kind of antelope) **ino a.**	**Lo-seru lo-ba la.**
Class XIV.		
Ganda.	**Ogu-ntu** * **ogu-mu gwa.**	**Agantu a-biri ga.**
Class XV. †		
Gisu.	**Gu-koko** (gigantic fowl) **gu-kwera gwa.**	**Gimikoko gibiri gya.**

We have seen that the root remains unaltered while the prefix changes for the plural. But more than this, a root may change its prefix for that of another class. **Umu-ntu** is "human being," but by exchanging its prefix for the 8th (in Zulu **ubu-**) it becomes an abstract noun **ubu-ntu,** "human nature." In some languages (not Zulu) it can, by taking the fourth prefix, come to mean "a thing"—*e.g.*, Nyanja **chi-ntu.** (It is true that the corresponding Zulu class-prefix makes a noun, **isi-ntu,** but this does not mean "a thing" but "the human race," "the totality of mankind"—apparently a kind of collective or abstract noun). And in some languages we have **pa-ntu** (with the locative preposition **pa**) meaning "place." As to what the root **ntu** means in itself, it is impossible to say. It has been suggested that it implies *speech* and that **umu-ntu** is "the speaker," but the existence of such words as **chintu** makes it difficult to believe this.

* This has a "depreciative" meaning: **oguntu** = "a great, gawky person or thing." It survives in Swahili, as has been pointed out to me by the Rev. W. E. Taylor, but has assumed a form resembling that of Class III., with the plural prefix of Class II.: **ji-tu,** "an ill-conditioned person," plural **mi-ji-tu.**

† This is the "augmentative" class. Traces of it survive in Swahili and Nyanja, but have become merged in the fifth class. Gisu, in less recent books called "Masaba," is a very archaic Bantu tongue, spoken in the neighbourhood of Mount Elgon.

The Bantu languages, as has been seen, differ from the Sudanian, in having a regular plural inflexion. They have no gender. Sex is indicated, when necessary, in the same ways as in the Sudanian family. In Zulu, we may, perhaps, note the beginnings of gender—for the termination **-kazi** (which, however, is not exclusively feminine, being sometimes used to indicate what is large or strong) is suffixed to nouns, as **inkosi-kazi** = "chief's wife," **indoda-kazi** = "daughter."

There are no case-inflexions (unless we count the locative suffix *-ni* used in some languages), but some pronouns have a distinct form for the object. The genitive follows its governing noun, and is connected with it by a particle meaning "of"—being the root **a** joined with the characteristic vowel of the class to which the *noun possessed* belongs.

Bantu verbs are usually of two syllables and end in *a*, those of more than two syllables are derived forms. There are a few monosyllables, most of them irregular or exceptional in some way, and among them are found the verbs that do not end in *a*—*e.g.*, **ti,** "to say."

The bare root-verb is found in the second person singular of the imperative, *e.g.*, **hamba,** "go!" (Zulu); **piga,** "strike!" (Swahili): **ku** is prefixed to this to form the infinitive. Most moods and tenses, except the Subjunctive (which changes final *a* to *e*) and the Perfect in **-ile** (which, however, indicates *state* rather than *time*), are built up by means of auxiliary verbs. These compound tenses are very numerous.

The *Derived Forms* of verbs are a very remarkable feature. They are not peculiar to Bantu, for they exist in Hebrew and Arabic, and there are traces of them in Latin and even in English. *Cf.* "fall" and "fell," "sit" and "set"—the second of each pair being really a *causative*, *i.e.*, "to fell," is "to cause to fall"; "to set," "to cause to sit." Here the difference of meaning is marked by a modification of the vowel, but in Latin it is expressed by a suffix.

All Latin grammars give lists of "frequentative," "desiderative," "inchoative" and "diminutive" verbs, which are rather curious and exceptional in the language as we know it. Such are **es-urio**, "I desire to eat" (from **edo**, "I eat"); **cal-esco**, "I begin to be warm," from **caleo**, "I am warm"; **clam-ito**, "I keep on shouting," from **clamo**, "I shout." We shall find these forms very fully developed in all primitive languages; as they advance to the higher stages, they acquire the power of expressing the same thing more easily and conveniently by means of separate words.* They are indicated in Bantu (like the Perfect, the Subjunctive Mood and the Negative Conjugation) by *terminations, not prefixes.*

Their number varies in different languages; originally there were at least eight or nine, but some have fallen into disuse. Sometimes a derived form keeps its place in a language when its root-verb has become obsolete, and acquires a meaning of its own. Such verbs are apparent exceptions to the rule that Bantu verb-roots are always of two syllables; but the termination shows their real character. Thus, there is a Zulu verb **ahlula,** meaning "to overcome," and also "to separate." By its form this would seem to be the reversive of a verb **ahla**, but there is no such verb in the language at present. It may have meant—unless **ahlula** has modified its meaning in getting separated from its root—"to join."

* Thus, in Kongo, **wankangulwishila** means "he caused to untie for him," thus expressing in one word what we break up into two verbs, besides prepositions and pronouns. This illustrates the difference between what are called *synthetic* and *analytic* languages; the former are like picture-writing or the Chinese characters, the latter like our alphabet, which, with a far smaller number of signs, is much more serviceable, as there is no limit to the number of combinations that may be produced from them.

As we are only devoting a chapter, and not a whole book, to the Bantu languages, it does not seem advisable to give a complete list of all the forms, but two or three of them may be mentioned.

The *Causative* usually ends in **-isa,** as **fa,** "die"; **fisa,** "make to die"; **hamba,** "go"; **hambisa,** "make to go" (Zulu).

The neuter-passive in **-eka** or **-ika** (sometimes **-akala**) indicates *a state*, or *the capacity for undergoing an action*, as **vunjika,** "to be broken"; **oneka,** "to be visible" (Swahili). The difference between this and the Passive is, that the latter is thought of as *the result of a definite act on the part of some one:* **kikombe kimevunjwa** means "the cup has been broken" (by A. or B.); but **kikombe kimevunjika,** "the cup is (in a state of being) broken."

The *Reversive*, as its name shows, *reverses* the action of the primary verb. **Funga,** "tie," **fungua,** "untie" (Swahili); **simba,** "plant," **simbula,** "dig up" (Ganda).

The *Reciprocal* ending in **-ana**: **tanda,** "love," **tandana,** "love one another" (Zulu).

A good example of a derived form having become an independent verb is found in the Swahili **anguka,** "fall." This is really a neuter-passive (or "Middle") form of **angua** which is, itself, the reversive of **anga,** "to hang up." This verb **anga** is no longer used in this sense,* though there is a noun **anga**, meaning "air" or "sky" (*i.e.*, "that which is suspended aloft"—it is used as the equivalent of "firmament" in the first chapter of Genesis); **angula (angua)**, the reversive of **anga,** would mean "to take down," and **anguka,** "to be taken down" = "to fall."

The Passive (which in all Bantu languages is formed by means of the suffix *-wa*) should be reckoned among the

* Mr. Taylor informs me that it is still current in a special sense, of wizards, who are said to float in the air ("levitate"); hence a wizard is called **mw-anga.**

Derived Forms; in fact they might just as well be called Voices. It is no objection to say that all the forms can be put into the passive,* for, theoretically, they can likewise be compounded with each other to almost any extent.

As many as four different forms may be united in the same word. Holman Bentley, after enumerating thirty-seven different forms derived from a single verb (**kanga**, "to tie"), says (*Dictionary and Grammar of the Kongo Language*, p. 641) that if all the possible combinations were added "the simple verb *kanga* would appear in more than three hundred forms, each to be conjugated in the regular manner and *actually in use*."

The Subjunctive was mentioned, a few paragraphs back, as having a characteristic termination; it is perhaps a little curious, when we remember the vowel changes of the Latin subjunctive, that this should be obtained by changing final *a* to *e*. The uses of the Bantu subjunctive are much what we should expect, with this addition that where several verbs occur in a sentence, all except the first are often put into the subjunctive, as though the mere sequence of the narrative made them in some sort dependent on the principal verb.

A striking peculiarity of the Bantu languages is the scarcity of real adjectives. Most languages possess a few. In Zulu the list of genuine roots is a very short one. These take the prefix of their noun, as was explained with regard to *omu-hle* in our specimen sentence. But many notions for which we require an adjective are expressed by a noun or a verb. In the former case, it is used with the possessive particle. Thus in Nyanja, "good" is **-a bwino**; "a good

* Except, of course, where the sense forbids it, as in the case of the neuter-passive. But combinations occur which would be impossible in any European language. Take the Zulu **uku-feliselwa**, "to be caused to die for," *i.e.*, "to have some one caused to die for you," not "for" in our sense but rather "from," or as the Irish say "on you" = "to be made a widow."

man," muntu wa bwino ; "to be bad" is **ku ipa** ; "a bad man," **muntu wa ku ipa** = "a man of being bad."

Two more points we must notice which are of importance to the structure of the Bantu languages. There are three demonstrative pronouns, each of which varies with the noun to which it refers, representing three degrees of nearness to or distance from the speaker. "This" means something which is close to you, "that" something at a distance but still in sight; * "that yonder," what is too far off to be seen at all.† The way in which these pronouns are built up from the noun prefixes is very interesting. In Swahili we have :—

1st Class.
Sing. (**mtu**) **hu-yu** = "this"; **hu-yo** = "that"; **yu-le** = "that yonder."
Pl. (**watu**) **ha-wa** = "these"; **ha-o** = "those"; **wa-le** = "those yonder."

2nd Class.
Sing. (**m-ti**) **hu-u** = "this"; **hu-o** = "that"; **u-le** = "that yonder."
Pl. (**mi-ti**) **hi-i** = "these"; **hi-yo** = "those"; **i-le** = "those yonder."

3rd Class.
Sing. (**j-ino**) **hi-li** = "this"; **hi-lo** = "that"; **li-le** = "that yonder," etc.

It will be seen that the second part of the word corresponding to "this" is the prefix (or part of the prefix) of its noun-class (or, if you like, the inseparable pronoun belonging to that class) ‡ preceded by its own *characteristic vowel, aspirated*. (It must be remembered that *li* represents the old third-class prefix, *i-li*, which has disappeared in Swahili.) The second changes the final vowel of the first to *o*; the third adds *le* to the pronoun. Thus the first

* Or sometimes "that near you" = Latin **iste**.

† Sometimes, merely, "distant both from me and you" = Latin **ille**.

‡ **Yu** is no longer used with a verb in Swahili, except in the Lamu and Mombasa dialects: **yu simeme**, "he has stood" (= "is standing"), **yuaja**, "he is coming"—for which at Zanzibar they would say, **a-me-simama, a-na-ku-ja.**

syllable of the third pronoun is the second syllable of the first, which might be diagrammatically represented thus :

4th Class.	**ki-ti**	**hi-ki**	**vi-ti**	**hi-vi**
	ki-ti	**ki-le**	**vi-ti**	**vi-le**

These three demonstratives seem to exist in all Bantu languages, though their composition varies (*e.g.*, in Nyanja, the third is formed by the suffix **-ja ; u-yu, yu-ja**), and their exact significance may not be, in all cases, that given above ; *e.g.*, in some of the Congo languages "the form of the second position is used to describe an object near to the person addressed when that person is as far away as the voice will carry, and the third position is used of an object not more than ten feet away, if the object is in no particular relation to either person." *

The detailed discussion of these points must be reserved for a book devoted exclusively to Bantu grammar.

The Bantu languages seem to have almost unlimited powers of forming nouns from verbs—of which we may indicate a few. A noun denoting the *agent* is formed by putting the first-class prefix before the verb and sometimes (but not always) changing the final *a* to *i*. Thus, in Swahili, **kugema** is "to tap palms," † **m-gema** is "a palm-tapper," **ku-pika** is "to cook," **m-pishi** (from the causative **pisha**), "a cook." In Zulu **um-fundisi,** "a teacher," ‡ is from **fundisa** "to teach," **um-meli** "an advocate" from **mela** "to stand for" a person. (In Zulu nouns with this meaning sometimes have the fourth-class prefix **isi-** ; **isi-gijimi** "a messenger" from **gijima** "run" ; **isi-hambi** "a traveller" from **hamba** "go.") §

* Stapleton, *Comparative Handbook of Congo Languages*, p. 77.

† *I.e.*, to make incisions for collecting the juice which is drunk fermented as palm-wine or "toddy." It is a regular trade in the Coast districts of East Africa. There is a Swahili proverb, "If a tapper hears his palm-wine praised too often, he puts water into it."

‡ The usual word for "missionary."

§ The Zulu version of the *Pilgrim's Progress* is entitled **Ukuhamba Kwesihambi**, literally "the going of the goer."

Nouns denoting *actions* may either be the infinitive of the verb (ninth-class nouns) or they may change the final *a* into *o* and assume the fourth prefix (Swahili **ki-tendo** "an action," from **tenda** "do"), or the third plural prefix (Swahili **mavao** "clothes,"* from **vaa** "to put on," **ma-zao** "produce" from **zaa** "to bring forth")—the singular of these last, if in use, would have the prefix **u-**. **U-** (**bu-**, **ubu-**) forms abstract or collective nouns (Swahili **u-baya** "badness," from **baya** "bad"; Zulu **ubu-hle** "goodness," "beauty," **ubu-nja** "boorishness, insolence," from **i-nja** "a dog"). We have already mentioned its use to denote a country, as **Bu-ganda.** The fourth prefix generally (but not always) indicates the language of the people to whose name it is prefixed—originally it seems to have implied something like "sort" or "kind"; **se-Sutu** "of the Sutu kind" (*à la* Sutu), **ki-Swahili** "after the Swahili fashion," and even now its use is not exclusively confined to languages. This prefix is also used to denote the thing by means of which an action is performed, as **isi-hlalo** (Zulu) "seat," from **hlala** "sit."

A conspicuous feature in most, if not all, of the Bantu languages are the *Lautbilder* or "interjectional roots," of which some account was given in the last chapter. Monsieur Junod (Ronga) calls them "descriptive adverbs"; Dr. Hetherwick (Yao and Nyanja) "onomatopoetic adverbials"; the late Mr. Stapleton (Congo) "onomatopoetic vocables," and Bishop Colenso† "particles used adverbially," which, he adds, "are oftentimes a fragment of a verb." In reality the reverse appears to be the case: verbs are sometimes formed from these particles which, in themselves, like the monosyllabic roots in Tshi and Ewe, are quite invariable, though not always monosyllabic.

They are sometimes imitation of *sounds*, as **kuputu** "expressive of galloping"—**chum** and **pabva**, the sounds

* More usually **ma-vazi.** † *First Steps in Zulu*, p. 128.

made by something falling into the water, **pio pio,** the sound of beating with a switch ("swishing"), **ka ka,** or **ba ba ba,** blows of heavy sticks, etc., etc. But, and this ought to be particularly noted, they express *not only sound*, but *motion* (or the absence of it), *form, position* and even *colour.*

Thus, in Nyanja, **pyu** means "red," **pe** "silence," **bi** "black" (prolonged for emphasis: "the people were sitting **biiiii** = "the place was perfectly black with them"), **piringu,** "swarming," or "confusion" ("multitudes of rats running about **piringu piringu**"). In Zulu, **nya** "utterly"; **ufile wati nya,** "he is dead saying **nya**"="dead as a door-nail"; **yima uti twi,** "stand upright" (saying **twi**)—"he broke a stick so that it said **poqo**" (snapped). We need not multiply examples; the important point is to make out whether these particles have ever given rise to verbs —and I think there is evidence that they have.

For instance in Zulu, we have **bobo,** expressive of piercing a hole through anything—*e.g.*, a piece of wood. **Ukuti bobo** is "to make a hole," or "to be pierced with a hole," but we also have the verb **boboza** "pierce," and its intransitive form **boboka** and the noun **im-bobo** "a hole." In Ronga * we have **ku nyupela** "to throw oneself into the water," from **nyupe,** which is described as the sound of "a man falling into a lake." This seems more likely than that **bobo** and **nyupe** are "fragments of verbs." Colenso, in a passage subsequent to the one previously quoted, says that while some of these "adverbial forms" have been derived from verbs "others are probably imitations of the sound referred to." He was unaware of the prominent position occupied

* See *Elementary Grammar of the Thonga-Shangaan Language,* by the Rev. H. A. Junod of the Swiss Mission (Transvaal and Portuguese East Africa). Thonga is a term covering several distinct languages, one of which, Ronga, is spoken by a tribe living near Delagoa Bay.

by these particles in other Bantu languages,* some of which have only been reduced to writing since his time, and it does not seem to have occurred to him, or to others then engaged in the study of these languages that the imitation is *not confined to sound.*

The possible origin of the Bantu languages will be discussed in Chapter VI., after we have taken a brief survey of the Hamitic family.

THE PRINCIPAL BANTU LANGUAGES. (*See Map.*)

I. South of the Zambezi.

Zulu.	Kalanga.	Sutu.	Herero.
Ronga.	Chwana.	Xosa.	Ndonga.

II. **East Africa.**

Pokomo.	Gikuyu.	Nyoro.	Makua.
Swahili.	Ganda.	Nyamwezi.	Yao
Giryama.	Gisu.	Shambala.	Gogo.

III. West and Central Africa.

Duala.	Lolo.	Lunda.	Konde.
Benga.	Mbundu.	Luyi.	Nyanja
Kongo.	Luba.	Ila.	Bemba.
Bangi.			

BANTU TEXTS

1. NYANJA.

Pa-na[1]-li [2] kalulu ndi kamba, ndipo
There were (a) hare and (a) tortoise, and
a[3]-na-lima m'munda wao wa nzama, ndipo
they cultivated in garden their of beans, and
a-na-pika nzama, ndipo kalulu a-na-ti, "Ndi-nka
they cooked beans, and (the) Hare said, "I go

* Bleek does not seem to have noticed it. But his great work on Bantu Grammar was far from complete when he died.

m'tengo, u-ka-mva [4] ku-lira [5] u-tawe." [6]
into (the) bush, if you hear crying-out, you run-away."

Ndipo kalulu a-na-nka, na-lira,[7] ndipo kamba
And hare he went and cried-out, and tortoise

a-na-tawa, ndipo kalulu a-na-dza, na-dya nzama
he ran-away, and (the) Hare he came and ate beans

zija.[8] Ndipo kalulu a-na-itana,[9] na-ti,
those. And (the) Hare he called and said,

"Kamba, ta-dza!" [10] ndipo kamba a-na-dza,
"Tortoise, come!" and (the) tortoise he came

ndipo kalulu a-na-ti: "A-dya nzama
and (the) hare he said: "He eats beans

zija nkondo"; [11] koma a-na-ti wo-chenjera [12]
those (the) war"; but he said cheating

kalulu. Ndipo kalulu a-na-lima ntedza,
(the) hare. And (the) hare he cultivated ground-nuts,

ndipo kamba a-na-lowa m'tumba
and (the) tortoise he entered into (the) bag

la ntedza, na-dya ndipo kalulu
of ground-nuts and ate (them), and (the) hare

a-na-itana kamba, ndipo kamba a-na-bvomera,[13]
he called (the) tortoise, and (the) tortoise he answered,

ndipo kalulu a-na-ang'ana m'tumba la
and (the) hare he looked in (the) bag of

ntedza, a-na-m-peza kamba
ground-nuts, he him found (the) tortoise

m'menemo [14] a-ta-dya [15]
in that same (place) he had completely eaten

ntedza, ndipo kalulu a-na-tawa na-lira.
(the) ground-nuts, and (the) hare he ran-away and cried.

[Notes 1 to 15 will be found on pp. 74, 75.]

*The Same in I.P.A. Script.**

pa'nali kalu:lu na ka:mba, ndipo anali:ma m mu:nda wao wa nza:ma, ndipo anapi:ka nza:ma ndipo kalu:lu anati " diŋka mtɛŋgo, ukamva kuli:ra uta:we." ndipo kalu:lu anaŋka nali:ra, ndipo ka:mba anata:wa, ndipo kalu:lu anadza, nadja nza:ma zidja. ndipo kalu:lu anaitana, nati " ka:mba tadza," ndipo ka:mba anadza ndipo kalu:lu anati " a:dja nza:ma zi:dja ŋkɔndo; kɔma anati wɔtʃendʒɛra kalu:lu. ndipo kalu:lu anali:ma ntɛdza ndipo ka:mba analɔwa m tu:mba la ntɛdza, nadja, ndipo kalu:lu anaita:na ka:mba, ndipo ka:mba anabvomɛra, ndipo kalu:lu anaaŋana m tu:mba la ntɛdza, anampɛza ka:mba m mɛnemo atadja ntɛdza, ndipo kalu:lu anata:wa nali:ra.

NOTES.

1 *Na*, particle indicating past tense.

2 Verb "to be."

3 *A*- pronoun, third person singular. Past tense of *lima* "cultivate."

4 *u*- pronoun of second person singular. *Ka* particle equivalent to "if" and "when."

5 Infinitive (used as a noun) of *lira* "cry."

6 Subjunctive, used as imperative.

7 For *ni* (= *ndi* = "and") *a-lira* = "and he cries."

8 "Remote demonstrative" agreeing with *nzama*, which is a plural of the third class.

9 Properly a reciprocal, but the simple form *ita* is not used in this language, though it is *e.g.* in Swahili.

10 The prefix *ta* is used to form an "immediate imperative," otherwise this mood is (in the singular) the unaltered root of the verb.

11 That is "the enemy"; *nkondo* is properly of the third class, but it takes the first class pronoun because personified.

12 A kind of participle, contracted from *wa-ku-chenjera*, which is

---

* This transcription is approximate only, the nature of all the Nyanja sounds not having been completely determined.

the infinitive with the possessive particle prefixed to it; literally "of being clever," or "of cleverness."

[13] Applied form of a verb *bvoma*, which is not in use, though it exists in Zulu as *vuma* = "agree." Originally, therefore, it would mean "to give an affirmative answer."

[14] A "relative demonstrative" pronoun, being the root *mene*= "the same," with the class-pronoun (in this case the locative in the sense of "in") prefixed and suffixed to it.

[15] *Ta*="finish" is here an auxiliary indicating completion.

Connected Translation.

Once upon a time, the Hare and the Tortoise cultivated a bean-patch together; and (when the beans were ripe) they cooked them. The Hare said, "I am going away into the bush; if you hear any one calling out while I am gone, you must run away." He went away and cried out (when he was out of sight), and the Tortoise ran away. The Hare came out from his hiding-place and called to the Tortoise to come back and then told him that a war-party of the enemy had come and eaten up all the food. But this was only said to deceive him. The Hare then planted ground-nuts, and the Tortoise crawled into the bag of nuts (which he had left lying on the ground) and ate them. The Hare (not seeing the Tortoise), called to him, and the Tortoise answered; the Hare then looked inside the bag and found the Tortoise, who had finished eating the nuts. So the Hare ran away, and cried (with vexation).

2. Ganda.

As the sounds of Ganda are not yet satisfactorily fixed according to the I.P.A. system, no transcript into that alphabet has been attempted. In the following text (taken from the *Manuel de langue Luganda*, published by the French missionaries in 1894) the orthography of the C.M.S. has been followed.

Musaja[1] ya-funa[2] mbuzi-ze[3] nyingi; na-funa
(A) man obtained goats his many; and he obtained
omu-'du[4]-we eli-nya-lye ye Sikilyamunaku.
slave his name his he Sikilyamunaku.

E-ngo, ne-ja, n-e-lya mbuzi-ze zona
A leopard and it comes and it eats goats his all
ne-leka-o[5] e-mbuzi-ye e-mu gy-a-singa
and it leaves there goat his one which he surpasses
okwāgala. Na-gamba omu'du-we nti: Embuzi
to love. And he says (to) slave his, saying: "Goat
yange eno o-gi-lunda-nga,[6] o-gy-etegereze.[7]
my this thou it herd continually, thou it look-after.
E-nsolo bw- e-li-'ja[8] ne-mala e-gi-kwata,[9]
(A) wild-beast when it shall come and it finishes it it seizes,
na-we, Sikilyamunaku, to-'da-nga[10] mu nyumba
and thou, Sikilyamunaku, do-not return ever into house
yange; o-genda-nga mu nsiko ensolo
my; thou, go-away entirely into the bush (the) wild-beast
ne-ku-lya." Ne wa-ita-o[11] 'naku[12] ntono
and it thee eats." And there pass where days few
omu'du na-imbula embuzi ku mu-gwa,
(the) slave and he unties the goat from the cord,
na-gi-twala ku 'tale, na-gi-sibikirira
and he it takes to (the) pasture, and he it tethered
ku mugwa om-wamvu na-tula wa-nsi.
by (a) cord long and he sits on ground.
Embuzi ne-lya omu-'do. Engo neja
Goat and it eats grass. Leopard and it comes
n-e-kwata embuzi, ne-walula ne Sikilyamunaku
and it seizes (the) goat, and it pulls and Sikilyamunaku
na-walula. Engo ne-singa ama-nyi
and he pulls. Leopard and it surpasses (in) strength
ne-twala embuzi, ne Sikilyamunaku
and it carries-off goat, and Sikilyamunaku

ne-mu-twala mu kibira ; ne-tula
and it him carries-off into forest ; and it sits down
ne-lya embuzi. Ne Sikilyamunaku na-tula
and it eats goat. And Sikilyamunaku and he sits down
wa-nsi. Engo ne-buza Sikilyamunaku nti :
on ground. Leopard and it asks Sikilyamunaku saying:
" Eki-ku-lese[13] kiki ? To-n-tya
"That which thee has-brought what? Dost-thou-not me fear
ku-ku-lya ? " Sikilyamunaku na-gamba : Mukama wange,
to thee eat ? " Sikilyamunaku and he says : Master my
e-ya-n-funa,[14] ye yafuna nembuzi
he-who me obtained he he obtained also (a) goat
eyo gyo-lya, na-n-gamba, nti :
that which thou eatest, and he (to) me said, saying:
Embuzi yange eno e-sigade[15] emu ; Sikilyamunaku,
Goat my this it remains one ; Sikilyamunaku,
o-gi-lunda-nga, o-gyekanya-nga.' "
thou it herd continually. thou it look-after continually.' "

NOTES.

[1] With the initial vowel: *omu-saja*, " man " (male).

[2] The inseparable pronoun of the third person is *a*, but before a vowel it is *y*. The past tense has *-a-* prefixed to the root ; the third person is therefore *y-a-funa*, instead of *a-a-funa*.

[3] In Ganda, as in some other languages, shortened forms are used for the possessives of the second and third persons : *wo* for *waku*, *we* for *wake*, etc.

[4] This is an example of a word containing a " long consonant." By some (*e.g.* by the French Fathers) it would be written *omuddu*. No satisfactory phonetic account has yet been given of these consonants.

[5] This *-o* (for *-wo*) is an " affix of place." It is classed among relative particles. *-e* is the pronoun used both for *embuzi* and *engo* strictly according to their grammatical class : in some languages they would be treated as persons and take a first-class pronoun.

[6] *gi* is the object-pronoun for the *n* class, the subject-pronoun being *e*. It is very unusual to find subject and object pronouns

different in any class but the first; but Ganda has preserved some primitive features lost elsewhere. *-nga*, suffixed to a verb means "utterly, completely," in a prohibition it is equivalent to "never."

[7] *gi* here becomes *gy* because the verb-stem begins with a vowel. *Cf.* also in last line *ogyekanyanga*. It is not the objective relative *gye*, which occurs in the last line but one (*gya-singa*). *E-tegereza* is properly a reflexive verb, which, in its simple form, means "listen to." The addition of the reflexive pronoun often modifies the meaning to a certain extent; and the actual force of the pronoun is sometimes lost sight of, which would account for the double pronoun. Two object-pronouns together are very unusual in most Bantu languages—not, apparently, in Ganda.

[8] *Bwe* is a particle meaning "when." "It is the Objective Relative form in agreement with *obu-de* ('time of day') understood; *lit.* 'the time of day *on which*'" (*Elements of Luganda Grammar*, p. 95). *Li* is the sign of the future.

[9] *E-*, subject-pronoun, agreeing with *ensolo*; *-gi-*, object-pronoun, agreeing with *embuzi*.

[10] *-to-* is the negative particle used with the imperative and with the second person singular in the present and some other tenses; *-nga* makes the prohibition a general one: *to'danga* "never return!" *Tontya*, farther down, is the indicative present negative, "dost thou not fear me?"—the infixed *n* being the object-pronoun of the first person.

[11] *Wa* is the preposition found in most languages as *pa*; here almost gone out of use, except as a locative particle; *-wo* is its corresponding relative suffix. *Wa-ita-o*, "there passed there," that is, "when there (had) passed," or, more literally, "(in the place) where there (had) passed."

[12] *'naku* for *e(zi)nnaku*, plural of *olu-naku*.

[13] *lese*, perfect of *leta*.

[14] *e-* is the relative prefix.

[15] *sigade*, perfect of *sigala*, "remain."

The prefixes have not been hyphened throughout, as they can easily be recognized after a few repetitions.

3. Chwana.

(*Serolong Dialect.*)

The following transcript was made by Mr. Daniel Jones. The pronunciation recorded is that of Mr. Solomon Tshekisho Plaatje, a Rolong native of Mafeking.

Unaspirated **p, t, tʃ** and **k** are also pronounced **p', t', tʃ'** and **k'**, especially when emphasized.

k tends to become **c** ("palatal" plosive) before front vowels.

tl is used provisionally to represent a **t** exploded laterally with simultaneous glottal closure. It strikes the ear as a single sound.

w following a consonant letter in this text is used to represent a labialized and velarized form of that consonant; thus **rw** does not mean **r** and **w** pronounced separately, but a combination of the two (lips rounded *during* the **r**). Similarly **ɥ** is to be pronounced simultaneously with the sound written immediately before it.* (New letters are not used for these labialized sounds on account of the large number that would be required.)

ə represents an extremely short **e**.

The tones are represented as follows:—

high-level,	**ā**.
mid-level	unmarked.
low-level,	**a̱**.
high-falling,	**à**.
low-falling,	**a̖**.

The tones of **m, n, ŋ, r** may be significant. These sounds must be taken to have essential tones whenever final or followed by a consonant. Thus the first **n** in **xon̄ne** and the **ŋ** in **naŋ̄** have high-level tone; the **ŋ** in **leɾātshiŋ**, the **m** in **xōmpie:nō,** and the first **m** in **mmē** have mid-level tone; the **ŋ**'s in **lexodīmò:ŋ̱** and **thāɛ̄lo̖:ŋ̱** have low-level tone.

↓ is used to indicate that all following tones in the sentence are slightly lower than the corresponding tones in the preceding part of the sentence.

Vowels having the low-level tone are often completely devocalized.

* **ɥ** is the consonantal sound of French *u* in *puis*.

THE LORD'S PRAYER.

ra:rā ŏā ro:nā:, ĕō ʊ̄ kwā lexodīmò:ŋ̱; leīna ɟā xā:xo ā ✓lī itshēphīsì:we̱. pūʃɔ ĕā xā:xo ā ì:tle̱. thā:tɔ ĕā xā:xo ā ī dīrwɛ:, mōnʊ̄ leꜰātshiŋ ɟà:kā kwā lexodīmò:ŋ̱. ō re ꜰɛ̄ xōmpīe:nō seɟɔ̄ sā ro:nā sā mālạ:tsi̱. ō rē itʃɥhārɛ̄:lɛ̄ melatō ĕā ro:nā ɟà:kā rē itʃɥhārɛ̄:✓lā bā bā naŋ̄ lī mēlatō lī rọ:na̱. ō sɪ rē x̄xɛ̄:lɛ: mō thāɛ̄lọ:ŋ̱; mmė ō re xʊ̄lʊ̄le mō bʊʃulè:ŋ̱. xon̄ne sā xā:xo īlī pū:✓ʃɔ̄, lē thā:tā, lē kxalalɛlɔ, kā: bo sēna bʊkhụ:tlɔ.

CHAPTER V.

THE HAMITIC LANGUAGES.

The term Hamitic as here applied is derived from the tenth chapter of Genesis, which embodies a very ancient and valuable record of ethnological tradition. This has been very generally misunderstood, through the supposed necessity of making it account for all the races in the world. The most probable view seems to be that it only applies to the three races then known to be inhabiting the shores of the Mediterranean, who radiated from that central sea over the three continents; so that, roughly speaking, the descendants of Shem might be supposed to occupy Asia, those of Ham Africa, and those of Japhet Europe.

America, of course, was quite outside the ken of those who compiled the record; but even in the Old World, the Dravidians of India, the Mongols, the Negros and other black and yellow peoples, were probably—if known at all—left outside the scheme of the nations, just as some of the South African Bantu, in relating how the human race (which means themselves) first made their appearance in the world, incidentally admit that the Bushmen were there already.

Nowhere can we find any statement that the "black" Africans are descended from Ham. To make Canaan their ancestor is a mere assumption, which contradicts everything recorded about Canaan's descendants. The amazing exegesis which, relying on this assumption, used "the curse of Canaan" as a justification for slavery, is now happily a thing of the past.

The sons of Ham are said to have been Cush, Mizraim, Phut and Canaan, which really means that the nations known by those names at the time when this document was written, were believed to be descended from a common ancestor.

Mizraim is a name for Egypt (still called *Misr* by the Arabs); Cush has been identified with various tribes on both sides of the Red Sea, and Phut may be the same as "Punt," a land which we know from Egyptian records to have been somewhere in the south—perhaps in Somaliland.

Canaan is a difficulty, because we know from inscriptions and other evidence that the Canaanites (Phœnicians) were closely akin to the Hebrews and spoke very nearly the same language. But there are two points to be considered which may help towards a solution.

1. The relations between the Hebrews and Canaanites, when they first came in contact after a long separation, were such that both very probably found it difficult to believe in their original kinship.

2. There are indications of a remote affinity between the two language-families respectively called Semitic and Hamitic, as if they had been one branch which only became subdivided at a period subsequent to its severance from the Indo-European (Japhetic) branch.

However that may be, the name Hamitic is now generally adopted as a convenient designation for a group of languages occupying a very important position in Northern Africa, and spoken by the people variously called "Berbers," Kabyles, and Moors; they really represent the Libyans, Mauritanians, and Numidians who occupied the country in Roman times.* They call themselves Amazirg or Imoshagh, which appears to mean "the free" and consist of a number of different tribes. One of these, the Zawia, or Zouaves, has become famous all over the world, through

* Cust, *Modern Languages of Africa*, i. 98.

giving its name to a division of the French army. Their existence was first discovered, in 1788, by Venture de Paradis, whose MSS. were published by the French Government in 1844, after the annexation of Algeria, and the language was further studied by Hodgson (American Consul at Algiers), by the late Professor Francis Newman, and others. It was long something of a puzzle; it was soon discovered to be akin to the language of ancient Egypt and its descendant, Koptic, which were then classed with the Semitic family and by some called "Hebræo-African" or similar strange names. As more and more languages were discovered, whose relationship to the above was evident, the similarity of structure growing clearer the more closely they were studied, Lepsius and Friedrich Müller became convinced that they ought to be placed by themselves in a "Hamitic Group," which they did not yet feel justified in calling a "Hamitic Family." This last step has been taken in quite recent years, and the characteristics of this family have been traced in a masterly manner, by Professor Meinhof in his book *Die Sprachen der Hamiten* (1911).

Fuller knowledge of these languages has solved several difficulties, *e.g.*, as to the proper position of Hausa and Masai.* Canon Robinson was perplexed by the presence of more Semitic elements in Hausa than could be accounted for by the mere importation of Arabic loan-words, while the bulk of the language was so plainly non-Semitic. Further examination shows that it is an inflected language possessing grammatical gender and having other points in common with both Hamitic and Semitic usage, while much of its

* Some important authorities, notably Sir Harry Johnston, differ as to the position of Masai. But it may safely be assumed as far as the purpose of this book is concerned—with the reservation that the question is not definitely settled. For the present it is sufficient to note that it is distinguished from the Sudan languages by having true inflections and from the Bantu by the possession of grammatical gender.

vocabulary belongs to the Sudanian stock, and the loss of some grammatical forms shows Sudanian influence. The best authorities have concluded that it should be classed as a Hamitic language: those points which had been regarded as Semitic can be referred to the element common to these two great families before their separation. The position of the genitive in Hausa is the Hamitic one—after its governing noun (as in Bantu). The verb usually follows its subject, as in Sudanian; only a few verbs keep the Hamitic position before the noun.

Masai and Nama, too, are Hamitic languages spoken by immigrant tribes (in both instances cattle-keeping nomads) who appear to have come from the north-east and penetrated—the latter to the southern extremity of the continent, the former to the neighbourhood of the Great Lakes. Both peoples had their language strongly influenced by that of the previous inhabitants with whom they came in contact: the Nama and other "Hottentot" tribes by the Bushmen, the Masai by whatever people they found in possession, whether Sudanian or Bantu.

Other Hamitic tribes are the Somali in the "Eastern Horn" of Africa, and the Galla.

Some of these last are found in Abyssinia and the deserts south of it, and others, a dwindling remnant, in the region between the Tana and the Sabaki. In the early part of the last century their raids extended to the Taita hills, and their chiefs levied tribute on the Arab governor of Takaungu. But, for the last fifty years or so, their activities have been circumscribed by the Masai on one side and the Somali on the other, and they have subsided into peaceful herdsmen and cattle-dealers, driving their beasts down from time to time to little coast towns like Mambrui, where they find purchasers in the Shehri butchers and Indian milkmen. In the intervals they migrate backwards and forwards between their summer and winter (or rather wet and dry season) pastures, in the steppes west of the Tana.

The Somali, too, are more or less nomadic, ranging with their cattle and camels as far as the left (eastern) bank of the Tana, and diversifying life by occasional raids on each other, with which, as a rule, the Government does not interfere, so long as they refrain from attacking inoffensive outsiders, such as the Bantu Pokomo. These, a tribe of fishermen and cultivators, long went in terror of their lives by reason of the " Wakatwa " (their name for the Somali), and I have been told that old people call the Milky Way "the road of the Wakatwa," because it stretches across the sky from north-east to south-west, in the direction from which the raiders used to come.

With all their ferocity, there is something engaging about the Somali—there always is, to the unregenerate mind, about a people who love raiding and horses, and make songs about them. One singer addresses his bay pony :

> " O Hamar, your strength ! as a black-maned lion,
> And a bull oryx with broad neck,
> And a bull rhinoceros !
> O Hamar, your obedience !
> The path which I desire your heart understands,
> As a dutiful wife, and an elder gone on a pilgrimage without grumbling ! "

Another says :

> " My fine horse, your colour, is it not white ? . . .
> Where camels graze, with you I must attack,
> And until I get my share I will not loosen girths."
>
> (Kirk's *Somali Grammar.*)

I fancy that Alan Breck would have appreciated these poets.

The Somali, probably, are very much the same sort of people as the ancient Numidians and Mauretanians (from whom the present-day " Berbers " are descended) except that the latter appear to have had more tribal cohesion and to have formed something like settled states. Several of their kings have left names in history: Hiempsal, who wrote a history of his people * (unfortunately lost), Masinissa, Jugurtha, that gallant raider and something more, who held the Roman armies in check for years and died at last, of cold and hunger, in a dungeon of the Capitol.

People of the same stock as these old Numidians and Libyans are the Shilha (or Shlu) of Morocco, the Zénaga of Senegambia, the Tawarek ("Tuareg") of the Sahara (who use a written character called "Tifinag"),† and the Guanches,‡ the extinct aborigines of the Canary Islands, who have left their mummied dead in the all but inaccessible caves of Teneriffe and Gomera.

The Fulbe, or Fulani of West Africa, of whom we shall have more to say in the next chapter, are also nomadic herdsmen. They are Hamitic by race and language, but their language stands, in a sense, by itself; it seems to belong to a more primitive stage than any existing Hamitic speech, and to have preserved some very ancient forms which, as we shall see, may help to explain a good many puzzles.

* This was written, not in his own Libyan language, but in Punic, which seems to have been as generally used, in his day, by North Africans, as English is by educated natives of the Gold Coast. At a later date, St. Augustine speaks of Punic as the language of the country people in what is now Algeria and Tunis, though by then it was giving place to Latin. As to the lurid picture drawn of Jugurtha by the Roman historian Sallust (practically our only authority), it is no doubt about as trustworthy as the official contemporary accounts of Cetshwayo's character. The crimes laid to his charge are of the kind usually committed by potentates whose territory it has for one reason or another been found desirable to annex. It is the old story of the man and the lion: the lions have been badly off for sculptors—and chroniclers.

† A modification of the old Libyan character, which has been preserved in numerous inscriptions, though they have not as yet been satisfactorily interpreted.

‡ The present (Spanish-speaking) population of the islands are partly descended from these.

Let us now look a little more closely at the main characteristics of this family. We have already seen that it consists of *inflected* languages.

Nouns usually express their relations of *number, gender and case* by *suffixes.*

Verbs form their *conjugations, voices, moods and tenses* by both *prefixes and suffixes.*

Like the Semitic and Bantu, the Hamitic languages have several *derivative forms,* or *conjugations* of verbs.

In Somali, *e.g.*, there are Intensive, Reflexive, Attributive and Causative forms. The causative suffix is *-si,* in Galla *isa* and in Saho * *-is* or *-ish,* which is interesting, when we remember that the commonest causative ending in Bantu is *-isa,* or *-isha.* Some of these derivatives are formed by *reduplication* (*i.e.*, by repeating the whole, or part of the root) as Somali **lab,** "fold," **lablab,** "fold up repeatedly," **goi,** "cut," **gogoi,** "cut in pieces"; or by *change of vowel*: Somali **gal,** "go in," **geli,** "put in." As in Bantu, these derivatives can be combined with each other to an indefinite extent. The Northern Hamitic languages are more copious in this respect than the Semitic, the southern (Fula, Nama) still more so, but none of them equal the Bantu.

Sometimes there is a suffix indicating the Passive, but some languages, such as Ancient Egyptian, Hausa and Somali do not use the Passive at all. "I am struck," *e.g.*, has to be expressed by "they strike me."

Tenses, as in the Semitic languages, express, not so much *time* as *complete and incomplete action,* contrasting, say, "action" and "state" or "movement, activity" and "result of activity." The idea of time, however, has come in later, and a number of tenses are formed, as in modern Arabic, by means of auxiliary verbs.

* Spoken in the Italian colony of Eritrea, between the Abyssinian mountains and the Red Sea.

To illustrate the formation of tenses, I subjoin an example:—

		Somali.	Saho.
		Sheg—" tell."	**Rab**—" die."
		Present (also called " Aorist " or " Imperfect ").	
Singular.—	1 p.	Sheg-a	rab-a
	2 p.	sheg-ta	rab-ta
	3 p.	sheg-a, f. sheg-ta	rab-a, f. rab-ta
Plural.—	1 p.	sheg-na	rab-na
	2 p.	sheg-tan	rab-tan
	3 p.	sheg-an	rab-an

For the Perfect, Somali has the suffixes: -ei, -tei, -ei (f. -tei), -nei, -ten, -en. Compound tenses are formed with **dona** " want," **jira** " be accustomed," etc. (as **shegi jira** " I am accustomed to tell ").

It will be noticed that there is a distinct form for the third person singular feminine, and that this is the same as the second person singular, as in Hebrew and Arabic, where, however, the second person is also found in both genders.

As a general rule, we may say that the plural of nouns is formed by suffixes: thus, we have, in Somali, **aba** " father," plural **abyal**; **fas** " axe," plural **fasas**; Galla, **woran** " spear," plural **woran-an**; Saho, **alsa** " mouth," plural **als-it**; **iko** " tooth," plural **iko-k**. But while there is no object in detailing the plural suffixes of all the various languages, we must not pass over a very curious phenomenon: the existence of different *kinds of plurals, not merely different ways of forming the plural.* There is a " distributive " plural, in which each of the things enumerated retains its separate individuality, and a " collective " plural in which they are massed into a unity. Then there is the case of things which are first perceived or named in the mass, as it were, and only afterwards, on reflection, sorted out into their separate particles: grass, milk, hair, water, minute animals which appear in swarms, etc. In this case, the original word is plural; a singular is formed from it by means of a suffix, and, later, a collective plural by a different suffix.

In Khamir (a Hamitic language of North Abyssinia), we find :—

Bil, "moths."	**Bil-a**, "moth."	**Bil-le**, "swarms of moths."
Lis, "tears."	**Lis-a**, "a tear."	**Lis-se**, "floods of tears."

This "collective" resembles the "general" plural in Bilin,* which denotes, not a plurality of individuals, but a plurality of classes or species: for instance, **dimmū-rā** is "a cat," **dimmu-t** "several cats," but **dimmū** is "a kind of cat," forming the plural **dima-mu** "kinds of cats."

Traces of these formations seem to survive in some of the Bantu languages, *e.g.*, Chwana, which has one plural denoting merely "more than one" of a thing, another to mean "a great quantity" of it. (**nku,** pl. **linku,** is "sheep," but **manku** "many sheep.")

The *dual number* still survives in Nama, and there are traces of it in Shilha. The Bantu languages, like the modern European ones, have dropped it entirely. It belongs to the stage of thought when it is not yet perceived that "one" and "more than one" are categories which include the whole existing universe—everything that is not one is more than one and *vice versâ*,† but "twoness" and even "threeness" are regarded as special conditions needing a separate designation.

Case is expressed by inflexions in the Hamitic languages. Sometimes the *subject* takes a suffix, as in Kafa, but usually it seems to be the unaltered form of the noun to which the inflexions for the other cases are added. Somali distinguishes it by the determinative particles **ba, ya,** which,

* The Bilin are a tribe living west of Masawa (the Italian port on the Red Sea) and called by their neighbours Bogos.

† Some of the Melanesian languages have four numbers: singular, dual, "trial," and plural.

however, are not suffixed and may even be separated from it by another verb, as **inanti ugu yereid ya araktei,** "the youngest girl saw," where **ya** belongs to the noun **inanti,** "girl."

The object is sometimes denoted by the suffix *-a* as in Nama

Khoib	**ta ǵawi**	**hâb-a.**
(The) man	rides	(the) horse.
Tita	**ra mu**	**Khoib-a.**
I	see	(the) man.

Sometimes a locative particle *-t* is suffixed.

Somali can prefix to the verb a pronoun representing the object, and Hausa changes the verb to show that an object is to follow. (These, of course, are not case-inflexions properly speaking.)

In Shilha, the *indirect object* has a distinguishing suffix, which does not seem to occur elsewhere. In Masai and Nama the dative case is sometimes indicated by the applied form of the verb; this, again, is not a case-inflexion.

The *Genitive*, which, as in Bantu, *follows its governing noun*, is usually marked by a special termination.

Galla.— **Wodes jila-t** =staff of ceremony.
Laf Orma-t =country of the Galla.

Somali.—**Nin magalo-da**=man of a town.
Akhal nin-ka =house of the man.

In Masai the genitive has a particle prefixed to it; *le* or *li* for the masculine, *e* for the feminine: **ol-alem le papa,** "the sword of the father"; **eng-aji e yeyo,** "the hut of the mother."

In Nama the particle *di* is used in something the same

way, but the position of the genitive is reversed—perhaps through the influence of Bushman speech:

Khoib di hāb.	**Taras di ‖ hoës.**
The man's horse.	The woman's milk-vessel.

A similar construction occurs in Masai, as well as the one already mentioned, thus "the ostrich chicks" may be either—

	'n-gera	**e-'sidai**
	the children	of the ostrich
or	**'n-e-'sidai**	**'n-gera**
	the-of-the-ostrich	the children

Masai has traces of locative forms and Nama of an instrumental case. But a complete declension with four case-endings nowhere exists.

All Hamitic languages distinguish a *masculine and a feminine gender*. There is *no neuter*. Nama, like old Egyptian, has "common" or "indeterminate" nouns which may be either masculine or feminine; these are sometimes wrongly called neuter.

Thus:—

Khoib "man," **Khois** "woman," { **Khoii** "person" (either man or woman).

There are various suffixes indicating gender, but, broadly speaking, we may say that the *guttural consonant* (K) is associated with the masculine, and the *dental consonant* (T) with the feminine.

Galla: **Kanke**, m. } thy
Tante, f. } (poss. pronoun).
Oboles-kia "my brother."
Oboleti-tich "my sister."
Jars "old man."
Jar-ti "old woman."

In Somali, the definite article is ***ki*** m., ***ti*** f., and is suffixed to nouns :

Nin-ki "the man," **nag-ti** "the woman," **walal-ki** "the brother," **walashi** (=**walal-ti**) "the sister."

In Hausa, the personal pronoun of the third person is, masculine **ya** "he," feminine **ta** "she." "Good" agreeing with a masculine noun is **nagari**, with a feminine **tagari**. Here the inflexions are prefixed.

It is remarkable that, in some languages, *e.g.*, Masai, Nama, Shilha and others, the inflexion which we call gender does not always serve to distinguish sex, but sometimes refers to relative size or importance.

"The Masai language," says Mr. Hollis,* "distinguishes by the article two genders or classes, answering approximately to masculine and feminine. As a general rule, the former signifies big, strong and masculine, whilst the latter may be taken to mean something of a weak or feminine nature, and also of a diminutive or affectionate character." In accordance with this principle, we find that the word for "sword" is masculine, when "knife" is feminine; "long coarse grass" is masculine, "short grass or turf" feminine, and so on.

In Nama **|huib** "a large rock" is masculine, **|huis** "a stone" feminine; and similarly, we have **gõab**, m. "sword, large knife," **gõas**, f. "pocket knife," and **koab**, m. "elephant" (of either sex), **!õas**, f. "hare" (of either sex).

"These examples show that it was not the difference of sex which was originally thought of in Nama, but the distinction between large, strong and small, weak things. It was natural that in most cases male animals should be placed in the 'large' and female ones in the 'small' class." †

* *The Masai, their Language and Folk-lore*, p. 8.
† Meinhof, *Die Nama-Sprache*.

Connected with grammatical gender in the Hamitic languages is a very remarkable phenomenon, called by Professor Meinhof the *Law of Polarity*. This will be more fully examined in the next chapter, as some of the most striking peculiarities in Fula are due to it, and it has an important bearing on the history of language.

It is shown in Somali, for instance, by nouns reversing their gender in the plural. Thus (we have already seen that *ki* is the masculine article and *di* the feminine)—

> **Asho-di** = "day," pl. **ashoïn-ki.**
> **Hoyo-di** = "mother," pl. **hoyoïn-ki.**
> **Libahh-i** = "lion," pl. **libahhyo-di.**
> (for **libah-ki**)
> **Ilig-gi** = "tooth," pl. **ilko-di.**
> (for **ilig-ki**)

Sometimes nouns which by their nature should be feminine are found to be grammatically masculine, *e.g.*, in Bedauye, **sha'** "cow."

As the Bedauye * are a pastoral people, who live largely on milk, this is not a slip due to want of familiarity with cattle; but there is a very good reason for the apparent anomaly, as will be explained later on in connection with the fact mentioned just now, that grammatical gender is not always or primarily a distinction of sex.

We saw just now that the position of the genitive is the same as in Bantu and the reverse of that in the Sudanian languages. The order of the sentence, however, differs from both, the verb usually preceding its subject, though this is not invariably the case. As subject and object can be distinguished by their form, it is possible (as in Latin) to vary the order without affecting the meaning of the whole. The reason for the order generally preferred,

* North of Abyssinia, between the Nile and the Red Sea.

viz., Verb–Subject–Object, is, Professor Meinhof thinks, because the Hamitic mind was fixed on the *action* as the main point, while the Negro, in a sense more logical, insisted that there must be a subject before any action could be performed, in the same way as he makes the possessor precede the thing possessed.

Some Hamitic languages have, no doubt through outside influence, adopted the Sudanian order: Subject–Verb–Object. Somali, curiously enough, has the order: Subject–Object–Verb. This is the beginning of a Somali tale, literally translated.

"A Sultan there was, a son he had. The son his mother died. Then the Sultan a wife he married. The Sultan the pilgrimage made," etc.

The normal Hamitic order is exemplified in a Masai story,* part of which, rendered word for word, is as follows: "He-is-there formerly, the-hare, and-he-sits by-the-river, and-he-sees one day the-elephant. . . . And-he-says-to the-big-one who-carrying-is the-bag of-the-honey: 'Father, make-cross-me the-water, for I-am poor.' And-he-him says-to the-elephant: 'Come! mount the-back my.' And he-it-mounts the-hare, and-they-go. Now they-it-cross, and-he-eats the-hare the-honey of-the elephant, but not-they-know the-elephants to-say he-it-eating-is." That is: "A hare that lived near a river one day saw some elephants . . . he said to the biggest one, who was carrying a bag of honey, 'Father, carry me across, for I am a poor person.' The elephant told him to get on his back, and when he had climbed up they started. While they were crossing the river, the hare ate the elephant's honey, but the elephants did not know that he was eating it."

* Hollis, p. 107.

TEXTS.

1. HAUSA.

THE LORD'S PRAYER.*

Addu'ar Ubangiji.

ubammu wanda ke chikin sama, atsarkake sunanka; mulkinka shı zo: abin da ka.ke so a yi shi chikin duniya kamar yada a ke yinsa chikin sama. ka ba mu rananga abinchin yini. ka gafarta mana laifinmu kamar yada muna gafarta ma waḍanda su ke yi ma mu laifi, kada ka kai mu wurin jaraba, amma ka cheche mu daga shaitan: gama mulki da iko da girma naka ne har abada. amin.

NOTES AND ANALYSIS.

ubammu, our father. mu, 1st p. pl. inseparable poss. pron. **-nmu** is pronounced (and sometimes written) **-mmu**.

wanda ke, who art. The fuller form of expression would be **wanda ka ke**, lit. who thou art.

sama, heaven, is a borrowed Arabic word denoting the heavens or the firmament.

a tsarkake, let it be sanctified. **mu tsarkaka zuchiyarmu**, we cleanse our hearts.

The Hausa word **sarauta**, Kingdom, usually denotes the territory governed by a king, not the sovereignty of the king. To express this latter idea it is better to use the Arabic word **mulki**.

ayishi, let it be done. Passive imperative.

---

* Kindly supplied by Canon Robinson, who adds the following notes on pronunciation:—

ḍ represents a hard d, in the pronunciation of which the point of the tongue touches the edge of the upper teeth, it is almost dt and somewhat resembles the French or German t.

ḅ has an explosive sound, the difference between b and ḅ being similar to that between d and ḍ.

ḳ is a sub-palatal guttural k. The Hausa term for it is ḳam mairuwa, *i.e.* the watery k: it is so called because the person pronouncing this k puts his mouth into such a position that he appears to be shooting out water from his throat.

kamar yada, like as. **r**, the feminine form of the connective, is used instead of **n**, as **kama**, likeness, is feminine; the expression **kaman yada** (or **yada**) is, however, frequently heard.

a ke yinsa, lit. let there be its doing. The prefix **ake** is used to denote the passive of the continuous present.

rananga, this day. **rana**, day; demonstrative pronoun **-nga.**

abinchin yini, the food of to-day. **yini** is frequently used as a verb, meaning to stay at a place for a day.

ka gafarta, thou didst forgive. **gafarta**, to forgive or excuse; cf. **gafara**, pardon!

ma mu, to us.

wurin, lit. the place of, is very commonly used as a preposition.

jaraba, trial or temptation.

har (or **hal**) **abada**, for ever, from Arabic أَبَدٌ eternity.

The following is a text in I.P.A. script. The passage is from Mr. F. W. H. Migeod's *Grammar of the Hausa Language* (London, 1914), and the transcription was kindly made by Mr. Daniel Jones, from the pronunciation of two European speakers of Hausa, one English and one German. As the transcription is not made from the pronunciation of a native, it cannot be guaranteed accurate in every detail.

a tʃikin kwɑːnakin dɑː akwɔi wʌni mai-duːkja dɛawa. a tʃikin koːwʌne bʌbam birni jɛna da aboːkan-ʃagali. wɔta rɑːna ja tɑːʃi za ʃi wʌni gari domiɲ ja duːba aboːkinsa a tʃã. sɛi ja d'ʌuki zab'iːra ja zuba guraːsa dɛ dabiːno a tʃiki. ja kiraoː ijaːlinsa, suka ji bãkwaːna; ja kaːma haɲa. ana nã jɛna tʃikin tɛfiːa, sɛi raːna ta faːra jin zaːfi. ja ga kua bʌbã inua, ja raːtse, ja zamna k'alk'aʃinta. bajanda ja ʃa inua ja d'ʌuko guraːsa dɛ dabiːno, jɛna tʃi jɛna ʃan ruːa. ja dʒe garin ʃi jɛs dɛ k'waːran dabiːno. sɛi ja dʒeːfa akã d'ã sɛrkin aldʒanu. ja faːd'i, ja mutu nan dɛ nã, gama inuar matataran aldʒanu tʃe. sɛi sɛrkin aldʒanu ja bajana ga mutumən nan dɛ takobi a ædreː ja tʃe masa, ka taːʃi iŋ kaʃeː ka kamar jɛda ka kaʃe d'ɑːna. mutumən nan fa ja tʃe k'aːk'a na ji na kaʃe d'ãka? sɛrkin aldʒanu ja tʃe masa saʔanda ka tʃi dabiːno ka jɛs dɛ k'waɪra sɛi ta faɪd'a bisa d'ɑɪna, ja mutu. mutumən nan ja taɪʃi, ja faɪd'i a gaban sɛrkin aldʒanu ja tʃe, ka gaɪfarta mani. ja tʃe baɪbu, lalɛi ne in kaʃeɪ ka. mutumən nan ja ʃiga jĩ roɪk'o ga sɛrkin aldʒanu domiɲ ja bɛr ʃi ja koɪma gida.

Stress and Tone are not marked in the above text; they may be indicated by diacritics where necessary. The I.P.A. stress-mark is '. The I.P.A. recommends that tone-marks should be devised as far as possible so as to give a rough indication of the musical values of the tones. (Cf. p. 46.) They appear to be an important feature in Hausa, but not much is known about them at present.

ʌ is the sound of *u* in "but." ə is unstressed *e* in such words as "the," "moment," when not specially emphasized, in current speech.

ƶ denotes a labialized *z*; it is often taken by English people for ***zw***.

TRANSLATION.

In the days of old there was a certain very rich man. He had partners in every large city, and so, one day, he set out for a certain place, in order to see his friend there. So he took a wallet and put into it bread and dates; he then called his relatives together and took leave of them and set off. After a while, as he proceeded on his way, the sun began to be very hot, and, seeing a large shady place, he turned aside and sat under it. After sitting in the shade for a time, he took out his bread and dates, ate them and drank water. He went to throw away the date-stones, but, in throwing them, he hit the son of the King of the Jinn, who immediately fell down dead. (For this shady spot was the meeting-place of the Jinn.) Then the King of the Jinn appeared to this man with a drawn sword and said to him, "Rise, that I may kill you, as you killed my son." The man replied, "How have I killed your son?" The King of the Jinn said, "When you were eating dates and threw away a stone, it hit my son and he died." The man got up and fell down before the King of the Jinn and said, "Forgive me!" He answered, "Not so, I must kill you." The man began to entreat the King of the Jinn to let him return home.

2. Kabyle.

The only texts I have been able to procure are the British and Foreign Bible Society's version of S. John iii. 16, part of which has been transcribed into I.P.A. characters by M. Paul Passy, and the verse of a hymn, with M. Passy's translation into French. Both these transcripts are from *Le Maître Phonétique* for July–August, 1907. The first is very fragmentary, because M. Passy was unwilling to print more than he had checked often enough to feel quite certain of the sounds. The Bible Society's version seems to follow the French system of spelling, but it will be easily seen, by comparing it with the transcript, what sounds are really meant.

Alakhăter Rebbi iḣammel dounith armi d-ifka Emmi-s louaḣiḋ, íouakken koul ouin ioumenen yi-s our ifennou ara madhe, lamâna aḋ-isâou thouḋerth n'daim.—[*Ed.* 1906.]

The first part of the above, transcribed on the I.P.A. system.

ala'ʁɑːtər r̩b'bi i'ʜamməl du'niθ armi difka m̩mis lwaʜeð, iwakkən kul win.

verse d kã:tik

inna-jaʁ-d, inna-jaʁ-d, ɟbbi ʋəʋəθ ənaʁ,
'rɔːʜəθ, ʁəðəməθ gə θfərɑɪt iɪu assa'!
isəfk-aʁ imslain is aku aθn-naʁ,
akkagi antaʋaː ləʋʁe n siðn aisa.
anʁəðəm s eldʒəhəd, anʁəðəm s eldʒəhəd;
ansəʋər, anaɪus, anzal alamma juʁɑɪl-əd.

Fʀᴇɴᴄʜ Tʀᴀɴsʟᴀᴛɪᴏɴ ᴏꜰ ᴛʜᴇ ᴀʙᴏᴠᴇ
(in Phonetic characters).

i nu di, i nu di, djø nɔtrə pɛɪr, 'ale, travaje dɑ̃ ma vɪɲɪ ɔʒɔrdɥi'! i nu fo mɛtr ɛ̃ɪsi sa parɔl ɑ̃ pratik; nuz akɔ̃ɪplɪɪrɔ̃ avɛk ʒwɑ la vɔlɔ̃ɪte dy sɛɲœɪr ʒeɪzy. nu lytrɔ̃ avɛk fɔrs, nu lytrɔ̃ avɛk fɔrs, nu pasjɑ̃ɪtrɔ̃ ɑ̃ vɛjɑ̃, nu prɪɪrɔ̃ ʒysk a s k i rəvjɛn.

CHAPTER VI.

THE KEY TO THE BANTU LANGUAGES.

We have several times referred to the Fula language, and it is now time to give a few particulars about it. The people who speak it call themselves Ful-be (in the singular, Pulo *) and their language Fulfulde; they are comparatively few in number, but are spread over a large area of Western Africa. Most of them are found in the Sierra Leone Protectorate and French Guinea; there are also a considerable body of them on the Middle Niger (the Masina district); others in Gurma and in the region beyond the Niger bend towards the Sahara. Some are, like the Galla and Masai, nomadic cattle-herds; these are called, on the Gold Coast, the "Cow Fulani," they are tall, light-complexioned people, very much resembling the Galla. Some have settled down and taken to agriculture; these, in general, are much darker than the nomads, which Mr. Migeod explains by saying that the latter are too poor to acquire negro slave-wives, while the sedentary ones have mixed with the neighbouring populations.† The Fulbe, he says, "are to be met with in all shades from light brown to black."

* This curious plural will be explained in the course of the chapter. The name is found in a good many forms, some of them merely disguised by spelling. Mungo Park wrote "Foolahs or Pholeys." The Hausa call them "Fulani," the Kanuri, "Fellata," French writers, "Peul."

† A parallel to this is to be found in the East African Wakwafi—Masai who have settled down and taken to agriculture.

Into the disputed question of their origin and the history of their migrations, this is not the place to enter; but we may note that they are mentioned by the Arab historian Makrizi (who wrote during the first half of the fifteenth century), and were probably established in West Africa long before that. They were converted to Islam at some time during the eighteenth century, and, at the beginning of the nineteenth, overran a large extent of country and conquered the Hausa states, under the chief Othman Danfodio. This man's son, Muhammad Bello, was the Sultan of Sokoto visited by the travellers Denham, Clapperton and Oudney. The Fula empire lasted about a century, in fact till the establishment of British rule in 1900.

The Fulfulde (Fula) language is, for several reasons, extremely interesting. It seemed so peculiar and anomalous that, as already stated, Friedrich Müller thought it necessary to place it in a division by itself. Maurice Delafosse, perhaps the greatest French authority on West African languages, thinks that it is a Negro language which was adopted by the light-coloured invaders from the north,* just as the Bahima of the Great Lake region speak the language of the Bantu among whom they have settled. But Fula is not a language of the Sudanian type, as is quite evident when we compare its structure with that of Tshi or Ibo.

If, again, we compare it with Berber, Galla or Somali, we shall find some great and important differences. The explanation suggested by Professor Meinhof is that it represents a very old type of speech from which the existing Hamitic languages have arisen. To make this somewhat clearer, we might say, adopting a metaphor of relationship

* He thinks they came from Cyrenaica (now Tripoli) by way of Air (or Asben) and Twat, settled in the region west of Timbuktu, where they founded the kingdom of Masina, penetrated into the country south of the Senegal and afterwards again moved eastward.

referred to in our first chapter, that Fula is not the sister or the cousin of Berber or Somali, but the aunt—possibly the great-aunt, only the analogy must not be pressed too closely.

I should add that Sir H. H. Johnston strongly disagrees with this view, as will be made clear in his forthcoming work (see the Bibliography at the end of this book). But it does not much matter, for our present purpose, whether Fula is directly related to the Hamitic family or not; while its peculiarities throw so striking a light, both on the Bantu noun-classes and the seeming anomalies of Hamitic genders, that Meinhof's view as to the origin of grammatical gender furnishes a very satisfactory working hypothesis. It cannot very greatly mislead readers who have not gone beyond what is contained in this book; those able to carry their studies far enough to appreciate the grounds of controversy will be able to judge for themselves whether or not it is tenable. I should like to add that, for purposes of comparative study, it is well to have a thorough *inside* knowledge of at least one language to start from. A comprehensive survey and classification may be made from outside knowledge—as the average librarian classifies books—but this must be merely provisional till a sound basis for comparison is established. Nor is it necessary to know a great many languages *à fond*, for this sort of work is largely done by co-operation and division of labour.

Let us look at some of the main points in the structure of Fula. The most striking is a *twofold class-division applied to nouns*, the two systems being quite independent of each other.

1. There is no grammatical gender as we understand it, or as it is found in some of the languages discussed in the last chapter. Instead, all nouns are divided into four classes: Persons, Things, Augmentatives, Diminutives. Sex is expressed, if necessary, just as it is in the Sudanian

or Bantu languages—by using distinct words, or by adding the words for male and female.

The plural is formed *both by modification of the initial consonant and by suffix*, these changes taking place simultaneously in the same word. The suffix belongs to the second method of classification, so that we may disregard it for the present. Each of the four classes just given changes its consonant in accordance with a very remarkable law.

A. Names of persons, in the singular begin with a *stop*,* voiced or unvoiced, as **ko'do̱**, "stranger"; **gańo̱**, "enemy"; **pio̱o̱**, "archer"; **dimo**, "free man." In the plural, the stop becomes a *spirant*: **ho̱'be̱**, "strangers"; **wańwańbe**, "enemies"; **fio̱'be̱**, "archers"; **rim'be**, "free men."

B. Names of things begin with a *spirant* in the singular, and change it to a *stop* in the plural. **Hirke̱**, "saddle," plural **kirke̱**; **fābru**, "frog," plural **pa'bi**; **wordu**, "dog," plural **gordi**; **rulde̱**, "cloud," plural **dūlde̱**.

C. Augmentatives begin, in the singular, with a *nasalised stop* (*i.e.*, a "stopped" consonant preceded by *m* or *n*), the nasal is dropped in the plural: **mbalu**, "sheep," plural **bali**; **ngiro**, "pig," plural **girodji**.†

D. Diminutives reverse this formation, having no nasal in the singular, but prefixing it for the plural: **bāngel**, "a small monkey," plural **mbādoń**; **dawańgel**, "little dog," plural **ndawakoń**; **gorogel**, "chicken," plural **ngerokoń**.

* Or "explosive consonant." See table and notes at end of Chapter I. The words are given as spelt by Westermann, according to Meinhof's system;—they would be written as follows in International Phonetic script: Koʔdɔ, gaŋɔ, piɔɔ, dimɔ, hɔʔbe, waɲwaɲbe, fiɔʔbe, rimʔbe. The "glottal stop" is indicated in Meinhof's system by ': ń stands for the sound spelt *gn* in French (as in *ignorer*). It is not *quite* the sound of *ny* in "lanyard," but for practical purposes is often so written, though English people (who usually pronounce "Nyasa" in three syllables) continually need to be reminded that it is not the *ny* in "deny."

† *j* = ordinary English *y* in "yet"

2. Besides this, nouns are divided into a number of classes, *marked by different suffixes*. Of these some authorities reckon 35 (counting, as Bleek does, singular and plural as separate), others even more. But there are far fewer plural than singular classes, a great many of the latter taking the same plural suffix. And each class has its distinctive pronoun, which stands in a recognizable relation to the suffix. The *meaning* of the classes is far clearer than in Bantu; *i.e.*, each is distinctly confined to one particular kind of thing. The following table is not exhaustive, but will at least serve to give a general notion of what these classes are like:—

Persons.

Sing. **-o** : **Pul-o, gor-ko**, "man." Pronoun **on,**
Plural **-be** : **Ful-be, wor'-be.** Pronoun **'ben.***

Liquids.

Sing. **-am** : **ndi-am** "water," **kos-am** "milk."
Pronoun **-dam.**
Plural **-e** : **ndi-e, kos-e.** Pronoun **de.**†

Large Animals.

Sing. **-ba** : **mbab-ba** "ass." Pronoun **nga.**
Plural **-di** : **bam-di.** Pronoun **din.**‡

Verbal Nouns.

Sing. **-al** : **and-al** "knowledge," **bal-al** "help."
Pronoun **ngal.**
Plural **-e** : **and-e, bal-e.** Pronoun **de.**

* This coincides with the person class already mentioned (but is quite independent of it) and so takes the one plural sign at the beginning and the other at the end. Westermann thinks that the classification by suffixes is the older of the two.

† Nouns of this kind are usually treated in Bantu as plurals with no singular, *e.g.*, Zulu, **ama-nzi** "water," or, if they belong to any other class than the **li-ma**, as singulars with no plural, *e.g.*, **u(lu)-bisi** "milk," **u(bu)-tshwala** "beer."

‡ This, again, coincides with the augmentative class.

Trees.

Sing. **-hi** : **bale-hi** "ebony tree." Pronoun **ki**,
Plural **-dje** :* **bale-dje**. Pronoun **de**.

Things in the mass.†

Sing. **-re** : **djabe-re** "a palm-nut," **maro-re** "a grain of rice." Pronoun **nde**.

The suffix is dropped for the plural: **djabe** "palm-nuts," **maro** "rice."

The classes whose suffixes are **-ri** and **-ru** have somewhat the same meaning, though their concord-pronouns are different.

Locatives: **-de** or **-rde**, formed from verbs: **bopto-rde** "rubbish heap" (from **bopta** "to shovel up"), **flo-rde** "threshing-floor." Pronoun **rde**.

These classes are not found in any of the Hamitic languages, but they have left traces, which, without a knowledge of Fula, might not have been noticed, or might be regarded merely as inexplicable anomalies. Probably they supply the key to a somewhat puzzling phenomenon —the number and variety of plural terminations in Hausa, Somali, Saho, etc., etc.

The more we study Fula, the more we find that, under the surface (for the first impression is one of total dissimilarity) it shows a striking likeness, in some points, to

* In ordinary English spelling *dye*. Both Meinhof and the I.P.A. use *j* to represent (broadly speaking, for there are subtle differences between the same sound in English, French and German) an English consonantal *y*.

† That is, things which occur, or are thought of, in large quantities (palm-nuts are a staple crop and usually handled by the bushel, or its equivalent). Probably the plural is the older form, the singular to which was formed, when it became necessary to individualize one grain of rice, one palm-nut, etc., by adding a suffix. So **belle** (pl.) is "fat," **belle-ne** "a lump of fat," **kode** (pl.) "the stars" (*i.e.* the sky full of stars, as seen in the mass), **hode-re** "a star," **bake** (pl.) "clay," **bake-re** "a clod of clay," and so on. Some nouns of this class take a plural suffix, viz.: *nje* or *de*, with the pronoun *de*.

the structure of the Bantu tongues, and the resemblance will no doubt prove to be even greater, when the subject has been more closely examined. It was noticed by Westermann,* and Meinhof speaks even more decisively. "Correspondences between Fula and Bantu have been repeatedly pointed out, and the study of the former language tends more and more to produce the impression that it lies in the borderland between Bantu and the Hamitic languages, and that its investigation is likely to throw light on the structure of both these speech-groups." After enumerating the coincidences noticed by Westermann, he goes on to say that the phonology of Bantu and Fula is in many respects identical, and, further, shows a remarkable agreement in the use of formative elements. These remarks will be found in § 24 (pp. 210–219) of his essay on "The Significance of Fula in connection with the languages of Hamites, Semites, and Bantu" which appeared in Volume LXV. of the *Zeitschrift der deutschen morgenländischen Gesellschaft* (1911).

Of course it is impossible here to go fully into the question, but a few illustrations will make clear what is meant. The Bantu clearly distinguish a person-class from all other classes and mark it in the plural by the prefix *aba-* (*ba-*, *wa-*, *va-*, etc.). It is impossible not to be reminded of this when we find that in Fula the same office is performed by the suffix *-be*. The "liquids" class in Fula has the suffix *-am*, in Bantu the names of many, if not most liquids belong to the *li-ma* class and are plurals without a singular: Zulu **ama-nzi** "water" (Swahili **ma-ji, Chwana me-tsi**), **ama-si** "curdled milk," **ama-futa** "oil, fat," **ama-te** "spittle"; Swahili **ma-ziwa** "milk," **ma-sizi** "soot" (which, though not a liquid, comes under the same category), and so on. It is difficult, too, in the case of the word for "water" not

* *Handbuch der Ful-Sprache* (Berlin, 1909), see preface, p. iv, and footnotes on pp. 205–208.

to suppose that the original form of the roots *ndi*, *nzi*, *di* (in the Duala *ma-*, *di-*, *ba-*), *ji* (more correctly *dyi*) is the same; but this could not be determined without an exhaustive scrutiny of all existing forms.

Again, there is a certain resemblance, which must not, however, be pressed too far, between the Fula *-re*, *-ri*, and *-ru*, and the Bantu *li-* and *lu-* classes. All these to some extent include things not as a rule found singly: *cf.* Zulu **u(lu)bisi** "milk," **u(lu)nyele** "hair," **u(lu)tuli** "dust," Nyanja **lume** "dew" (usually found in the plural **mame**), **luzi** "string," **lupsya** "burnt grass," Ila (N.W. Rhodesia) **lubibi** "cream," **lukobo** "a flock of white birds." The *lu-* class, as we saw in the chapter on the Bantu languages, has the same plural prefix (**izin-**, **in-**, **n-**) as the *in-* class; probably, in the first instance, it had none of its own and adopted this, when one was needed. Occasionally (as we saw in **lume, mame**) it takes the *ma-* prefix, as being appropriated to liquids.

Though, as mentioned before, the meanings of the classes are much clearer in Fula than in Bantu, and it may be said, that, in general, each contains the names of one definite series of objects, this must not be taken too absolutely. Any reader who has the curiosity to examine Westermann's grammar for himself will find, in p. 208, that, though the meaning of the three classes (*-re*, *-ri*, *-ru*) is said to be the same, the *-ru* class contains such words as **goki-ru** "monkey," **dondo-ru** "leopard," **dundu-ru** "drum," **dunia-ru** "the world." The last, an Arabic word, took the suffix *-ru* in accordance with some phonetic law which made it the easiest form to pronounce, and was then placed in the *-ru* class by analogy. This would be all the more likely to happen as the word * must have been introduced comparatively late, for we know the Fulbe did not become

* It is generally used by Moslems as a religious term: "this world," or "this present world" as opposed to "the world to come."

Muhammadans till the eighteenth century, when the original meaning of the classes had been more or less forgotten. Perhaps the other words are imported terms or they may have undergone phonetic changes which, in a similar way, seemed to necessitate the suffix *-ru*. In Latin there is no reason inherent in the nature of things, why a table or a pen should be feminine; but once the principle had been established (to examine why is not our present business) that *a* was a feminine termination, *mensa* and *penna* were as a matter of course ranged among the feminines.

It is more intelligible why **buwa-ru** "little bird," **domru** "mouse," **nobru** "ear," **dizgoru** "sweet potato," should belong to the *-ru* class. Ears, like eyes (which in all the Bantu languages belong to the *li-ma* class), are first thought of as inseparable pairs; it is only after conscious reflection that the need of distinguishing them is felt. Perhaps no one ever talked of "one eye" till some person had lost one. "Sweet potatoes" would come under the same heading as palm-nuts, but the close *o* in the second syllable (like *o* in "stone," not like *ou* in "ought") seems to require *-ru*, not *-re* after it. And "little birds" present themselves in the first instance to the native consciousness, in the flocks and swarms which hover with shrill cries over the ripening grain, and keep all the boys and girls of the village hoarse with shouting and weary with banging sticks against any resonant surface that may be available.

The use of the concord pronoun reminds one strongly of Bantu, and—not to extend these remarks to undue length—there are some striking resemblances in the numerals; *o* and *u* are used in intransitive formations in a way which recalls the Bantu passive in *-wa*; and the series of three demonstrative pronouns, corresponding with the distance of the object from the speaker, is similar in both.

Sir Harry Johnston,* some years ago, expressed the view that Fula might supply the key to the origin of the Bantu languages. The same conclusion was reached independently by Meinhof, who sums it up as follows: "I have come to the conviction that the origin of the Bantu languages may most readily be explained by supposing that some language very similar to Fula appeared as the speech of a dominant race among Nigritian (=Sudanian) peoples and assimilated a Nigritian vocabulary (*Sprachgut*)."

At first sight the whole structure and tendency of prefix languages seems so opposed to that of suffix-using languages like our own and the other European ones, that we are inclined to reject as absurd the supposition that any language could ever exchange suffixes for prefixes. But Sir Harry Johnston has pointed out that we ourselves say both "lift up" and "uplift," "bringing-up" and "upbringing," and, though these suffixes are still movable, we have analogous cases where the prefix or suffix has lost its separate existence and forms part of an indissoluble compound, as in "misfit," originally "thing that fits amiss." We find a tendency this way in such a word as "uplift," which is regularly conjugated as a verb, though we do not say "to upbring."

But, apart from this, we have the interesting case of a Sudanian language in German East Africa, Mbugu, which has acquired, or is in course of acquiring, the Bantu class-prefixes, though its roots are decidedly non-Bantu. We may expect, moreover, that some light will be thrown on

* In *Liberia* (vol. i.). In his article on the Bantu languages in the *Encyclopædia Britannica*, he speaks more cautiously. "We have no clue at present to the exact birth-place of the Bantu, nor to the particular group of dialects or languages from which it sprang. . . . Perhaps in grammatical construction (suffixes taking the place of prefixes) Fula shows some resemblances; and Fula possesses the concord in a form considerably like that of the Bantu, as well as offering affinities in the numerals 3 and 4 and in a *few* nominal, pronominal and verbal roots."

the question by the further study of those "Bantoid" or "semi-Bantu" languages, such as Ekoi, which are to be found in the Kamerun territory.

We referred in the last chapter to the "Law of Polarity," an expression borrowed from physical science and referring to the well-known law in electricity and magnetism that like magnets repel while unlike magnets attract each other. We saw that, in Somali, for instance, masculine nouns became feminine in the plural, and we have just been considering a similar phenomenon in Fula. It is not confined to the Hamitic languages, for we find similar anomalous plurals in Hebrew and in Arabic, hitherto regarded, for the most part, as unaccountable exceptions.

Professor Meinhof's remarks on the way in which grammatical gender, as we have it, may have arisen through the action of this Law of Polarity, are exceedingly interesting. Originally, he thinks, people may have divided the whole universe—made a "dichotomy" of it, in philosophical language—into "persons" and "not persons" (or "things"). Thus, if any change takes place in a given object on which we fix our thoughts, so that its relation to its surroundings is no longer the same, and we want to remove it from its original class, there is only one other in which it can be placed. If we think of a person, no longer as one but as many, we feel that some change is imperative; and as a non-person must, by the terms of the question, be a *thing*, the plurality of persons is placed in the thing-class. Conversely, a plurality of things must be placed in the person-class. Again, the person-class, in the first instance, has no reference to sex. But, supposing we begin to consider persons from this point of view, and start with the assumption that a man is a person. Very well, then, what is a woman? Clearly she is not a man, so some other place must be found for her, and the only place available is the thing-class. And so, in course of time, the not-person class became feminine.

The principle also works the other way, as we saw in the case of the Bedauye people's masculine cow. A cow, being female, should be in the non-person class. But she is far too important to be reckoned a mere thing—she must be a person—and being a person, be a male.

Stating this in a slightly different way, we may say that it looks as if there had originally been two genders, common and neuter and the neuter ultimately became a feminine, or perhaps in some cases (not in Semitic or Hamitic) was divided into neuter and feminine. It seems to me that the existence of two mutually exclusive categories might be quite sufficient to bring about the result, and that there is no necessity to adduce arguments drawn from the inferior position of women among primitive races, as Professor Meinhof goes on to do in another passage, suggesting that they were placed in the "thing" class because they were despised. But, as a matter of fact, the position of women is, and has been, on the whole, favourable—in some cases exceptionally favourable—among the Hamitic peoples.

It is remarkable that, in Zulu, while the word for "human being" irrespective of sex, is (as we saw in the fourth chapter) **umu-ntu** (first class) the words for "man" as male (**indoda, induna**) belong to another class, which does not primarily contain the names of persons, while again, **um-fazi** "woman," **um-ke** "wife" belong to the first (or "person") class. This may be an instance of the principle working the other way round.

We can even find traces of this sort of thing in European languages—though not in English, owing to the very restricted form which grammatical gender has assumed. But in the Dutch "*het volk*," "*het leger*," and the German "*das Volk*," "*das Heer*," we find that a plurality of persons has become a thing, Again, in French, "*l'armée,*" "*l'assemblée*" are feminine, though composed of males. (French, of course, like Spanish and Italian, has no neuter.) This becomes intelligible by a reference to the Law of Polarity.

How deeply this idea has penetrated into the life and thought of the Hamites may be gathered from some very curious points in Nama speech and custom. Sons belong to the mother's family, daughters to that of the father, and each is named accordingly. The husband, speaking of himself and his wife, *uses the first person feminine dual pronoun;* the wife, in like manner, *the masculine dual.*

Besides the contrast between "person" and "thing," we have also that between "subject" and "object." Normally, the subject is a person and the object a thing.

Subject.	*Predicate.*	*Object.*
The man	breaks	the stone.

It is therefore placed in the "thing" class and usually distinguished by a suffixed particle, which seems to denote place and to correspond, roughly speaking, with the preposition "to." This, in some languages, takes the form *t*, *et*, or *te*,* which, perhaps, explains why *t* has become a feminine termination in the Hamitic languages. Originally, it had nothing to do with gender, only with the distinction between subject and object. The "masculine" object only acquired a suffix in later times, when it had been entirely forgotten that, by the nature of the case, an object could not be masculine, *i.e.*, belong to the person-class. In Bedauye, the masculine object often has no suffix at all—a phenomenon quite unintelligible without the clue just given. Almkvist, the Swedish traveller, whose researches

* As in Bedauye:

Nominative.	**fena dauri**	"a fine spear."
Accusative.	**fena-t dauri-t.**	

on this language have been so valuable, was puzzled by this "apparent preference for the feminine object."

The supposed process by which gender and case (*i.e.*, the distinction of subject and object) arose, may be illustrated by a diagram borrowed from Professor Meinhof's *Sprachen der Hamiten.*

Person ······························ ← ······························ Thing
Large thing — MASCULINE FEMININE — Small thing
Subject Object

The dotted line represents the return of the feminine to the person-class, as instanced by the Bedauye cow.

FULFULDE TEXT.

The following extract is taken from a version of S. Luke xv. 11–32, made by a young Pulo, Audu Hamadu of Sokoto, under the superintendence of Prof. Westermann, and printed in the latter's *Handbuch der Ful-Sprache* (pp. 263–4). In this extract (the pronunciation being indicated by the provisional I.P.A. transcript immediately following) the diacritic marks used by Westermann have been omitted, with the exception of the ' used to indicate the glottal stop. The spelling is the same in principle as that used for Bantu by the U.M.C.A. and the C.M.S.

LUKE xv. 11–15.

Go'do i[1] woni, omo wodi suka'be[2] 'di'do, arandedyo
Man and was, he has sons two, elder
minyi ; aman minyi wari,[3] o[4] wi'i baba
and younger ; but (the) younger came, he said (to) father
makko non: baba am, mi'do[5] yi'di[6] koka[7] yam
his thus : father my, I wish (that you should) give me
ngedal dyaudi[8] ma[9] ndi[10] am. Baba ma'be
share-of goods where it mine. Father their

sendani 'be dyaudi mũ'ũ,[11] **o hoki 'be. Ga'da**
divided (to) them goods his he gave them. After
bal'de[12] **se'da 'bi'i ko suka o hautindiri**[13]
days few son his younger he collected
dyaudi mũ'ũ. fu, soti 'di, o hotyi tyede makko,
goods his, all sold it, he took money his
o yehi[14] **gari bo'dundi ; 'don o bonidi**[15] **dyaudi makko fu,**
he went country far ; there he wasted goods his all,
o anditai[16] **dyango. Nde o henyi**
he did not think (of) to-morrow. So (when) he (had) finished
madyingo dyaudi makko fu, rafo mango
spending goods his all, hunger great
nati gari ndi ; kanko nde o fu'di soitugo[17]
came (to) country this ; he then he began having-want
ko-nyame.[18] **O yehi, o he'bi ne'do**[19] **gari ma'be;**
(of) food. He went, he found (a) man (in) country their
o dyodi to makko yaire go'o ; ga ga'da ne'do on
he stayed with him place one ; afterwards man this
lili mo o dura[20] **nyamata-lopedye**[21] **nder ladde.**[22]
sent him, he feeds pigs in bush.

The Same in I.P.A. Script.

gɔd'ɔ i woni, omo woıdi sukaıb'ɛ d'id'ɔ, arandɛı djɔ i miɲi; aman miɲi wari, o wiʔi baıba makkɔ non; baıba am, mid'o jid'i kokaı jam ŋgɛdal djaudi ma ndi am. baıba mab'ɛ sɛnd'ani b'ɛ djaudi mũʔũ, o hoki b'ɛ. gad'a bald'ɛ sɛd'a b'iʔi kɔ suka o hautindiri djaudi mũ'ũ fu, soti d'i, o hotji tjɛıdɛ makkɔ, o jɛhi gari bod'undi; d'ɔn o bonidi djaudi makkɔ fu, o anditaıi djaıŋgɔ. ndɛ o heɲi madjiŋgɔ djaudi makkɔ fu, rafɔ maŋgɔ nati gari ndi; kaŋko ndɛ o fud'i soituıgɔ ko-ɲaımɛ. o jehi, o heb'i nɛd'ɔ gari mab'ɛ; o djoːd'i to makkɔ jairɛ gɔʔɔ; ga gad'a nɛd'ɔ ɔn lili mɔ o dura ɲamata-lɔpɛı-djɛ ndɛr laddɛ.

NOTES.

[1] *i* connective particle, equivalent to "and," "so," "then," etc., but never the first word in a sentence.

[2] Plural of *suka* "child," "son."

[3] *wari* past tense of *wara* "come."

[4] *O* is the inseparable pronoun (third person singular), used before all tenses except the present, which takes *omo*.

[5] *mid'o,* inseparable pronoun of first person singular, used with present.

[6] *Yid'i,* like *wodi,* has the present ending in *i*.

[7] *koka* imperative of *hoka* "give." One form of imperative changes the initial consonant in the same way as is done for nouns.

[8] *Dyaudi,* plural of *dyaudiri,* originally "sheep" or "goats." (*Cf.* our "chattel" and "cattle.")

[9] *ma,* originally a noun meaning "place," is found in combination with some of the possessive pronouns (*e.g.*, *makko* "his" = *ma* + *ko* "(at) his place").

[10] *ndi* is the pronoun of the *-ri* class, to which *dyaudiri* belongs; the plural *dyaudi* has the pronoun *d'i*. Possibly (unless there is a clerical error in the text) *ndi* is used because *dyaudi* is treated as a singular.

[11] *makko* and *mũ'ũ* are used indifferently.

[12] *bal'de,* pl. of *walde* "day." The simple *d* of the singular changes into *'d* (*d* with glottal stop) for the plural.

[13] Derived form of *hawa* "meet." *Hauta* "cause to meet, unite," etc.; *hautindira* "collect, bring into one place, mix."

[14] *Yehi,* past of *yaha* "go."

[15] *Boni* (probably an original past used in a present sense) means "be bad," "make bad," "spoil." *Boni tyede* "waste money." *Bonidi* is the fifth conjugation, which takes the suffix *-da* in the present and *-di* in the past, and indicates that the action is performed completely, exhaustively—"he utterly wasted."

[16] *Anda* "know," third conjugation *andita* "think." *Andita-i* is the negative past, the final *a* being lengthened and *-i* suffixed.

[17] *Soit-ugo* a verbal noun formed by suffixing *-ugo*. It is a peculiarity of this class that it is always preceded by an auxiliary verb (*fu'da* "begin" is here practically an auxiliary).

[18] *ko-nyame,* lit. "something to eat." *Ko* is a sort of indefinite pronoun, very often compounded with verbs in this way (*e.g.*, *ko-hule* "something that frightens," from *hula* "frighten"); *nyama* "to eat." (*Cf.* the word *nyama* "meat," found in most Bantu languages.)

[19] *Ne'do,* pl. *him'be,* is "a person" (like the Bantu *mu-ntu*); *gorko,* pl. *wor'be,* is "a man" (not a woman).

[20] There does not seem to be anything corresponding to a subjunctive mood, and it is rare to find anything like a subordinate sentence.

[21] *nyama-ta-lopedye,* literally "eats not dirt," is properly the wild (bush) pig, as distinguished from the domestic pig. The translator seems to have been shy of mentioning the latter unclean animal!

[22] *ladde* = "bush" in the sense of "steppe, uncultivated land," etc., the place where swine would naturally be herded.

CHAPTER VII.

THE BUSHMAN LANGUAGES.

THE Bushmen are generally considered as the aborigines of South Africa,* and at one time seem to have spread over the whole southern extremity of the continent, till they were encroached on, first by the Hottentots, then by the Bantu, and lastly by the Europeans. They are now rapidly diminishing, though there are still several tribes in the north-western part of the Transvaal and in the Kalahari desert. They are essentially a hunting race, and have never taken either to cattle-keeping or agriculture; hence it becomes difficult for them to live at all when the settled population increases. Some of the earlier Bantu invaders, however, lived on friendly terms and even to a considerable extent intermarried with them, and thus we find people, like the Abatembu of Cape Colony, and some Bechwana clans, who are partly of Bushman blood, but entirely Bantu in language and habits. The same is probably the case with a large population of so-called Anyanja and Angoni in Nyasaland.

Interesting as they are from an anthropological point

* Skulls of an earlier race have been found in caves in Cape Colony, and the Hottentots, at the beginning of the last century, had a tradition that, when they first reached the country, there was a tribe of people living on the shore (hence called, in Cape Dutch, *Strandloopers*), who ate shell-fish and dead whales washed up on the beach. There are large shell-mounds of unknown antiquity at Mossel Bay and near East London, which were no doubt accumulated by these people.

of view, it is their language which mainly concerns us here, and I must be content with referring for further information to G. W. Stow's *Native Races of South Africa* and Miss Lloyd's *Bushman Folk-lore*, only remarking that a perusal of these works results in a very different mental picture from that of the degraded and bestial creature which the name "Bushman," I fear, suggests to most of us. The late Rev. John MacKenzie, whose experience extended over many years, thought highly of the Bushmen, and said that he never met one who was not thoughtful and intelligent, and well-informed on such matters as had come within his experience.

It is quite possible that the Bushmen are the "Troglodytes" mentioned by Herodotus, whose language was "like the squeaking of bats." They may at one time have overspread the whole of Africa; and we learn from Egyptian records that, more than once, officials were charged to send for a "pygmy" from the land of Punt (*i.e.*, probably a Bushman) to dance before Pharaoh. (Their agility, and their wonderful power of imitating the action of any animal they have seen, are well known.) Geologists have calculated (from the rate of wear of rocks on which figures have been carved) that they must have been living near the Orange River at least 2500 years ago. The question of their possible relationship with the Congo and other "Pygmies" (none of whom have yet been found speaking a language of their own), or with the Wasanye, Juwano and Waboni of East Africa is one I cannot attempt to discuss here. I do not know where the name Wa-Sanye comes from (the people so called by the Swahili call themselves and are called by the Galla Wat *); but it may be an older designation, surviving from a time before they

* The Zulus call the Bushmen *Aba-twa*; a similar name is applied by Central African Bantu to the Pygmies: and the Wapokomo of the Tana call the Wasanye *Wa-hwa* which is the same word.

became subject to the Galla; and it is certainly curious that the South African Bushmen were called San by the Hottentots (*i.e.*, "inhabitants" or "aborigines"). Their name for themselves seems to have been "Khuai,"* meaning "men," whence the Zulus call them *Izi-cwe*. But there are several distinct tribes, with names of their own.

It used to be thought that the Bushman language was so strange and difficult that no European could learn it, unless he had the chance of picking it up in childhood. But this is quite a mistake, perhaps favoured by the exceptional facility with which the Bushmen learn other languages. One of the early French missionaries, Arbousset, who collected a vocabulary about 1837, says:—

"Their language is harsh, broken, full of monosyllables, which are uttered with strong aspirations from the chest, and a guttural articulation as disagreeable as it is difficult. . . . It is not without reason that it has been said of them that they cluck like turkeys. . . . The clucks are especially found at the recurrence of a letter which is of a harsh guttural pronunciation. . . . As this horrible aspiration recurs incessantly in the mouth of the Bushmen, one is inclined to say that they bark rather than speak."

Dr. Bleek had his attention early directed to this very remarkable tongue, but, up to 1870, he had little, if any opportunity of examining it at first-hand, and was forced to omit it from his study of South African languages. In the First Part of his *Comparative Grammar* (published 1862) he says:—

"The *Bushman* tongue is as yet too insufficiently known to allow us to assign it to its proper place in a general classification of languages; but it seems to be clear that its relationship to the Hottentot language is, at least, very remote. In fact, the probability is that it will be

* Properly *!kui* (! represents the "cerebral click"), pl. *!ci*.

found to belong to what may be called the class of Genderless Languages."

After the Second Part of his *Grammar*, or rather the first section of the Second Part, had appeared, in 1869, he quite unexpectedly found himself able to command the services of several Bushmen, and laid aside the work which, as Dr. Theal says, "could be completed by some one else at a future time," for that which "if neglected then, could never be done at all. . . . knowing that in the few wild people left he had before him the fast-dying remnant of a primitive race, and that if any reliable record of that race was to be preserved, not a day must be lost in recording it."

It so happened that, at that time, some Bushmen who had been sentenced to penal servitude for sheep-stealing were working out their sentence on the Breakwater at Cape Town. "There were two in particular, whose terms of imprisonment had nearly expired, and who were physically unfit for hard labour. The Government permitted him to take these men to his own residence, on condition of locking them up at night until the remainder of their sentence had expired." *

However, they manifested so little desire to escape that the locking up became a mere formality; and in fact their whole behaviour showed that they were by no means dangerous criminals. They could hardly be expected to have developed a conscience on the subject of sheep-stealing, seeing that the game by which they lived had been exterminated or driven away from their accustomed haunts, and they might in many cases have starved but for the domestic animals which came in their way.

These Bushmen remained on with Dr. Bleek for some time after they had been made to understand that they were free to leave, and subsequently induced several of

* G. McCall Theal, in Introduction to Miss Lloyd's *Specimens of Bushman Folk-lore*, p. xxxiv.

their relations and friends to come for longer or shorter periods. Dr. Bleek and his sister-in-law, Miss Lloyd, who helped in the work, were enabled to learn two distinct Bushman dialects, and to take down from dictation an immense mass of matter, comprising tales, fables, traditions, accounts of Bushman customs, etc. Dr. Bleek was at work on a dictionary when he died suddenly, August 17th, 1875.

Some of the materials collected were published,* with a literal translation, by Miss Lloyd, who survived till July, 1914; but a great deal still remains to be printed. It is most interesting and important, from an anthropological as well as a linguistic point of view, as the Bushmen, unlike the Bantu, have a somewhat elaborate mythology, which, according to Bleek, has points of contact with that of the Australian aborigines. But this subject, as well as that of the paintings (sometimes really wonderful) which they have left in caves and rock-shelters in many parts of South Africa, lies beyond the scope of our present study.

The first Bushmen from whom Dr. Bleek obtained his material came from Strontbergen, a district south of the Orange River in the neighbourhood of Prieska, and about 350 miles north of Cape Town. They were followed by some from the Katkop mountains, north of Calvinia, about two hundred and fifty miles from Cape Town and nearly the same distance westward from the homes of the first set. However, it was found that the two sets could understand one another without difficulty.

At a later date, in 1879, Miss Lloyd secured the services of some lads belonging to the !Kuṅ (or !kũ) tribe, described as living "beyond Damaraland," and these could not understand, or make themselves understood by, the Cape Colony Bushmen. These "Kung" (as the name may be written for ordinary purposes) are still to be found in German South-West Africa, near the Okavango River and on the

* *Specimens of Bushman Folk-lore*, London, 1911.

"*zandveld*" near Grootfontein. A few words of their language were collected by Dr. Passarge, but more recently a German missionary, Herr Vedder, has published what appears to be an excellent grammar of it.*

Dr. Passarge says that "the Bushman race, though so uniform from an anthropological point of view, divides itself into a number of tribes speaking different languages, *i.e.*, languages in the strict sense, not merely dialects." He thinks there are two main stocks represented by the ‡Aukwe—they are called "Makankan" by the Bechwana—(speaking the same language as the Kung), and the ||Aikwe. Their respective areas meet about the middle of the Kalahari desert. The ‡Aukwe and ||Aikwe cannot understand each other's speech; in fact the two languages have hardly a word in common. Several other tribes are included with the ||Aikwe in the common designation of "Ng'ami Bushmen"; but we need not give their names here. Dr. Passarge has collected short vocabularies of six languages which, as they stand, are not very useful for comparison, and some sentences of ||Aikwe. The ‡Aukwe and Kung words, so far as I have been able to compare them, agree, on the whole, with the Kung texts collected by Miss Lloyd.

Dr. Bleek came to the conclusion that the Bushman languages are genderless, though, at one time, he appears to have thought that they had lost this feature rather than that they had never acquired it, and that they and the "Hottentot" languages were branches of a common stock which had diverged "at a remote period of some thousands of years." On this point, however, he speaks with extreme caution, and, in 1873, wrote as follows:—

"The Bushman literature most nearly resembles that of their neighbours the Hottentots, and also that of the most primitive mythological stages of other more northern nations, whose languages either are sex-denoting or may

* *Zeitschrift für Kolonialsprachen* (Hamburg), vol. i. Nos. 1, 2.

have branched off from the sex-denoting languages, losing the sex-denoting characteristics. To this latter class of languages the Bushman also seems to belong, and (in contradiction to the Hottentot, in which the gender of the nouns is everywhere clearly marked by the endings and maintained by the concord), it has no genders which have any reference to the distinctions of sex. If it ever were sex-denoting, it has now lost those signs of gender which so clearly mark the grammatical gender in Hottentot."

This agrees with what Vedder says, that there is no distinction of gender in pronouns, though there is one between *persons* and *things without life*, or *animals* : * the pronoun of the third person is, in the former case, **hà**, pl. **hasn**, in the latter **gà**, pl. **gàsn**.

Bleek seems to have been on the track of this distinction ; at least, such is, I think, the meaning of the following passage :—

" Instead of eight different forms for each pronoun, as in Hottentot, . . . the Bushman has only two forms, one which is only used in the singular (**ha** 'he, she, it,' **ā**, 'which, who, that') and another which is mainly used for the plural (**hi** 'they,' **ē** 'which, who, that'). I say purposely 'mainly used for the plural,' for, curiously enough, the plural form is frequently employed in Bushman, where we should use the singular, and where, in fact, the singular is indicated by the Bushman himself, by the addition of the first numeral, or some other clearly singular form. The fact seems to be that there are in Bushman two classes of nouns in the singular, viz., one which has the forms **ha** and **ā**, etc., for its corresponding pronouns, and the other with the forms **hi** and **ē**, whilst the plural of both

* The distinction drawn between persons and animals is curious and scarcely primitive ; though, in most Bantu languages, names of animals, as a rule, belong to other classes than the person-class. But in some, the logical mind insists on treating them as if they did belong to that class.

classes has only the one form for each pronoun, this being at the same time one which outwardly agrees with the second form of the singular. This is the only trace as yet found of that division of the nouns into classes which is effected by the concord." *

The difference in form between the above pronouns and the Kung ones given by Vedder is sufficiently accounted for by difference of dialect. The Kung, too, seem to use for the plural a suffix (**sa**) which can also be used by itself. The further discrepancy, which may be due either to insufficient knowledge or to difference of idiom, need not concern us here; the main point is that there is a distinction between two classes of nouns, which is only marked by means of their pronouns. Vedder, when he comes to treat of nouns, says that they have neither gender nor class.

Bleek calls the Bushman language "monosyllabic." † If this represents his matured opinion, it must be understood with the same qualifications as were suggested in our chapter on the Sudanian languages, for a glance over any page of Miss Lloyd's Bushman texts will show numerous words of two and some of three syllables. The greater number of the words in Dr. Passarge's vocabularies are of one syllable; *cf.* also **||kã̄**="lion," **sa**="eland," **ã̄n**="flesh," **!nu**="foot," **!há̄**="wife," or "husband," **hó**="to lift," **||kú**="hair," **hi** (or **hā̃**)="to eat," etc., etc.

But Dr. McCall Theal says: † "The roots of many Bushman words are apparently polysyllabic, thus marking a great difference from Hottentot, all of whose roots are monosyllabic. But it is possible that upon very close analysis some of these polysyllables might prove to be really composites," which is probably the case.

* Report concerning Researches into the Bushman Language and Customs, quoted in *Specimens of Bushman Folk-lore*, pp. 445, 446.

† *Specimens of Bushman Folk-lore*, p. 435.

It would of course be premature to make any definite statement as to the relationship, if any, between the Bushman and the Sudan languages; yet such relationship appears to me to be extremely probable. It would go far to explain what Dr. Bleek evidently regarded as a puzzle.

"In Bushman . . . the greatest irregularity prevails with regard to the forms of the plurals of the nouns, and from fifty to sixty different ways of forming the plural occur at the least, in this language. It seems as if the most original form here were a reduplication of the noun, and that this reduplication, together with the use of certain other particles or variations of the stem of the noun, has given rise to the great multiplicity of the forms."

"Variations of the stem of the noun" is probably a mistake; but the other two methods will be recognized as those used to form the plural in the Sudan languages. Turning to Herr Vedder's Grammar, we find that the Kung Bushmen form the plural by suffixing **sn**, the pronoun of the third person plural, as is done in Ewe, Kunama, etc. If the noun is followed by the numerals "two" and "three," the suffix is not used, and the noun itself undergoes no change.

The position of the genitive is the same as in the Sudan languages:—

Gaoχa dz'u	**‖Kã ga !nu**
Chief('s) house.	Lion's foot.

Bleek says there is a "suffixed genitive particle" (**ka**, **ga**, **ya** or **a**) which is indeclinable (see the last example), but does not seem to be necessary; in fact, the cases where it is omitted are more frequent than those in which it is used. (*Cf.* the use of **fe** in Ewe.) Vedder says that in Kung the genitive and its governing noun are simply juxtaposed without connection.

Another point of similarity with the monosyllabic West

African languages is that the same word may be used as a noun, verb or adjective:

gu=" road " and " to go."
ǂn=" word " and " to say."

There is no indication of case, which has to be expressed merely by position in the sentence.

There are no numerals beyond *three*, higher numbers are indicated by showing the fingers, or in some such way as this: " five elands over a ridge " might be described as " two lying down, one looking towards the water and two looking towards a particular hill."

In somewhat the same way, Galton remarked that the Nama and Herero know if one sheep or goat is missing out of a large flock—not by counting them, but because they are so familiar with each individual as at once to notice if any is absent.

The great difficulty in the way of connecting the Bushman languages with the Sudan family lies in their phonology, especially the famous " clicks " about which so much has been said and written. These are almost peculiar to Africa, and in Africa, with a few exceptions, to its southern extremity. There are four of these sounds in Nama: as these are the four most easily pronounced Bushman clicks, it seems pretty clear that the former adopted them from the latter, just as three of them (the " dental," " cerebral " and " lateral ") have passed from either Bushman or Hottentot into Zulu and Xosa, and one into Sesuto. Bleek found five clicks in the speech of the Cape Bushmen; Vedder gives six for that of the Kung.

These clicks are explained by Professor Meinhof as " suction-sounds " (*Sauglaute*) which, as may be proved by trying them, is obviously correct. The old theory that they were " sounds of inspiration," not of expiration, is untenable, for a click is often produced simultaneously with a stop, voiced or unvoiced, and as of course this sound is produced by emission of breath, it would follow that one had to breathe in and out at the same moment, which is impossible. The symbols used by Bleek and adopted by Meinhof and other recent German writers on the subject are as follows :—

| indicates the "dental click," which is produced by "pressing the tip of the tongue against the front teeth of the upper jaw, and then suddenly and forcibly withdrawing it," or, as Meinhof puts it, "making a suction-movement (*Saugbewegung*) with the tongue against the incisors." This click is represented in most Zulu books by **c**, as in "Cetshwayo."

! the "cerebral click," in which the tip of the tongue is curled up against the palate, and, as before, "suddenly and forcibly withdrawn." This is the click written *q* in Zulu, and heard in **i-qanda** "an egg," to be carefully distinguished from **i-kanda** "a (human) head."

|| the "lateral click," in which the tongue is withdrawn, as above, from the side teeth "on the right or left, or better still, from both sides at once" (Meinhof). This seems simpler than the directions given by Tindall, according to which it is "generally articulated by covering with the tongue the whole of the palate and producing the sound as far back as possible. . . . European learners, however, imitate the sound by placing the tongue against the side teeth and then withdrawing it," which also seems to be the current Zulu mode of pronunciation. "A similar sound is often made use of in urging forward a horse."

‡ "'the palatal click' is sounded by pressing the tip of the tongue with as flat a surface as possible against the termination of the palate at the gums and removing it," as before. This click is called by Meinhof "alveolar," and his directions are, "to lay the relaxed tongue against the gums and then forcibly remove the front part" (not merely the

tip, though apparently this may be used alternatively) "while the rest remains quiet." "This difficult click," says Bleek, "is rarely, if ever, employed in Kafir (*i.e.*, Xosa) and Zulu words," but there seem to be some doubtful examples in the former, spelt by Boyce in his *Dictionary* with *qc*.

⊙ the labial click "sounds like a kiss." (I do not know if this is the same as the labial click described by Wuras,* "to articulate which the tongue moves very quickly, like that of a performer on the flute.") This is not given by Vedder, but he has a second lateral, marked |||, thus agreeing with Miss Lloyd's observations, for she found that the Kung Bushmen did not use the labial click, and pronounced the lateral in a slightly different manner. As the signs for the two pronunciations of the lateral click occur side by side in her Kung texts, it is probably by an oversight that she states these people to have only four clicks.

Bleek mentions at least two other peculiar sounds in Bushman, described as "a strong" and "a gentle croaking in the throat," but one of these appears to be identical with Vedder's "guttural click." It is unnecessary to say any more about them here. The main point is that, so far as at present ascertained, these, as well as the clicks, are not found in the Sudan languages. Does this necessarily prove that they are not related ?

This question can only be settled (1) by an exhaustive comparison of roots, and (2) by ascertaining whether any language which once possessed clicks has ever lost them.

No one is in a position to solve either of these problems at present ; but a hint of the lines along which a solution must be sought, is contained in a note by Sir Harry Johnston.†

"In the Pygmies of the north-eastern corner of the

* See Bleek, *Comparative Grammar*, p. 14.

† *Journal of the Royal Anthropological Institute*, July-December, 1913, vol. xliii. p. 380.

Congo basin and amongst the Bantu tribes of the Equatorial East African coast there is a tendency to faucal gasps" (*i.e.*, the glottal stop) "and explosive consonants, which suggests the vanishing influence of clicks."

To this I may add the following :—It has proved very difficult to find out what, if any, Bantu sounds correspond to the Bushman clicks, probably because the Zulu words in which they occur are borrowed Hottentot or Bushman roots, which have not spread into other Bantu languages. Yet I have been able to trace a few in Chinyanja, and in these the click is usually replaced by the "velar nasal" (sometimes called "ringing *ng* and written *ng'* or *ṅ*), as **n|cane** (**-ncane**)=**ṅono** (**-ng'ono**) "small." This sound appears to be quite common in the Sudan languages. It is a little difficult for Europeans to pronounce when it occurs at the beginning of a word, as in **ng'ombe, ng'oma,** etc.

There is one click-language, the Sandawi, recorded from East Africa, but, up to the present, little is known of it. Sir Harry Johnston says it is "of undecided affinities . . . spoken by a cattle-keeping, semi-nomad tribe, to the south of the Victoria Nyanza. . . . The existence of clicks in this language is undoubted, but I have not been able to trace much affinity in word-roots between (it) and either Bushman or Hottentot, though it is noteworthy that the word for four, **haχa**, is almost identical with the word for four in all the Hottentot dialects, while the phonology of the language is reminiscent of Bushman in its nasals and gutturals."

Recent investigations, however, reveal the possibility that Sandawi (and some other apparently perishing languages in the depression west of Kilimanjaro, such as Mbulunge and Ngomwia) may be really Hamitic. If so, the case may be parallel with that of Nama.

Statements which have been made as to some other languages containing clicks (see Cust's *Modern Languages of Africa*, vol. ii., pp. 436, 437, and Bleek, *Comp. Gram.*, p. 14), must be received with caution, as it is not certain that genuine clicks (*i.e.* suction-sounds) are meant. What is referred to as a click in Galla is probably the glottal stop (which sometimes does produce a click, but belongs to an entirely different order of sounds); and it must surely be a mistake to say that Krapf observed it in Swahili. The Zulu sound called by Bleek a "faucal explosive," has sometimes been denominated a click, but, I think, without sufficient reason.

All these sounds may, as Sir Harry Johnston suggests, have originated from clicks, but the language and locality in which they occur should be taken into consideration. The same sound may be found in two different languages, but it will not necessarily have arisen in the same way; *e.g.*, the Galla glottal stop need not be supposed to represent a vanished click, while a glottal stop in a Sudanian language might very probably do so.

The value of the collections made by Dr. Bleek and Miss Lloyd can hardly be over-estimated, because there are now very few, if any, people left who speak the dialect of the Cape Bushman. Some of the Kung and other tribes, as we have seen, still survive in the Kalahari desert; but most of the Bushmen to be found in Cape Colony to-day know little or nothing of their own language and traditions. These, or more probably their parents, were kidnapped in childhood by unscrupulous farmers (who not unfrequently took this method of supplying themselves with herd-boys), and readily picked up Cape Dutch, or whatever speech they came most in contact with, completely forgetting their own.

The history of the Bushmen is, like that of the Tasmanian aborigines, a blot on the fame of the white race. It is no doubt inevitable, that hunting tribes must suffer, in one way or another, as a country becomes more settled; and the Bushmen suffered a good deal at the hands of the peoples by whom they were partly driven out before the arrival of Europeans. But there has been much cruelty and injustice which might and should have been avoided, and the fact is all the more lamentable when we learn from those who have known them best that they are really an interesting and attractive race, with many fine qualities.

However, it may be some little comfort to reflect that their disappearance has not in every case meant extinction; many of them, as already stated, seem to have been peaceably absorbed into thriving Bantu populations.

CHAPTER VIII.

THE SEMITIC FAMILY.

FOR the sake of completeness, and because Arabic is a very important medium of communication through about a third of the African continent, we must now devote a few pages to the Semitic languages.

Of this family, the languages longest settled in Africa are to be found in Abyssinia. The Abyssinians, as is well known, have been Christians since the fourth century; and the Bible was translated into Ethiopic or "Ge'ez," still the liturgical language of the country, though no longer spoken by the people—certainly before the seventh. This language is akin both to Hebrew and Arabic, though its closest resemblance is not with the Arabic of the Koran so much as with a very ancient dialect of Southern Arabia, called Sabaean (or, less correctly, Himyaritic) and known to us through inscriptions dating back as far as 800 B.C.

Abyssinia was very early colonised by settlers from Yemen. It is not known when this migration took place, but probably it was accomplished in a series of movements extending over a considerable period. In this way the Semitic immigrants would become incorporated with an original Hamitic population; and such—with the addition of a strain of negro blood—is, in the opinion of anthropologists, the composition of the Abyssinian people.

The kingdom of Axum (whose capital is still the sacred city of the Abyssinians), flourished from the first to the seventh century, A.D., and was converted to Christianity about 450. A number of inscriptions have been found there, both in Greek and Ethiopic, the latter being particularly interesting as showing different stages of the language.

This Ethiopic character differs from both Hebrew and Arabic in being written from left to right, and also in another respect which will be mentioned later on. It is still used for writing Amharic, which has been, since the end of the thirteenth century, the official language of the court and government.

At that period, the central province, Amhara, obtained a sort of predominance which was maintained, on the whole, up to the nineteenth century, and the Emperor (his proper title is **Negus Negesti** "king of kings") had his capital at Gondar. The late Emperor Menelek, who was chief of Shoa, fixed his residence, after he had attained to the overlordship, at Adis Abeba, the present capital.

But Amharic, though it has thus succeeded to the position of the ancient Ethiopic language, is not its direct representative. It contains a great many elements which are probably Hamitic, and some have denied its right to rank as a Semitic language at all. It is gradually absorbing the Agau dialects; while the Galla of the Yejju and Wollo districts have also adopted it in place of their own speech. Amharic, says Nöldeke, "has diverged from the ancient Semitic type to a far greater extent" than any of the other languages included in that family. "Many of the old formations preserved in Ge'ez are completely modified in Amharic."

The modern representative of Ge'ez is Tigre, spoken in the northern province of Abyssinia, in which Axum is situated, in fact, it may be said roughly to correspond to the ancient Axumite kingdom, though part of the latter is now included in the Italian colony of Eritrea. When there is a doubt about the meaning of any old word,

Abyssinians explain it by a reference to Tigre. Though not altogether free from foreign influences, it may be considered, in the main, as purely Semitic. It, or a dialect of it, is also spoken in the Arkiko district, within the Italian colony.

Other Semitic languages in this part of Africa are those of Harar and Gurague. The latter is spoken by a small tribe of Christians, isolated in the hill-country south of Shoa, the former in the little Emirate of Harar, which, conquered in the sixteenth century by Muhammad Granj, became Moslem and, in its entire separation from the parent country, developed its Abyssinian dialect into a new language.

Another Semitic language, introduced into Africa at a later period than Ethiopic, but now quite extinct, is Punic or Carthaginian. It seems to have been widely used in North Africa, almost more so than one would expect, considering that for a long time the Phœnicians only planted trading stations along the coast (comparable with the West African settlements of Europeans in more recent days), and even at the height of their power, did not extend very far inland. In St. Augustine's time * (the beginning of the fifth century, A.D.) it was spoken by the country people near Hippo, and, in writing to the Pope about the consecration of a bishop for the new see of Fussala, he lays stress on the importance of choosing a man familiar with Punic. It seems to have been the first language he himself heard or spoke, though he says that he picked up Latin very early, in play as it were, and without any of the torment and misery which Greek afterwards cost him at school.

It is not to be supposed that all the people who spoke Punic were necessarily Carthaginians; some of them were "Libyphœnicians," a mixed race descended from the

* He died in 430, at the age of seventy-five.

Phœnician immigrants and the Libyan natives; and no doubt it had also been adopted by a considerable number of the pure aborigines. A similar phenomenon may be observed to-day on the Gold Coast, where numbers, not only of half-castes but of pure-bred natives, habitually speak and write English, and bear English names, sometimes inherited through several generations. (There has of late years been a movement towards the resumption of Tshi and Fanti.)

That Augustine really meant Phœnician when he speaks of "Punic" and not (as some have suggested) * Libyan or "Berber," is evident from several passages, where he dwells on the close similarity between this language and Hebrew.

But even in his time, it was, at least in some parts of the country, giving way to Latin. In one of his sermons he quotes an ancient and well-known proverb, "which I will tell you in Latin, because you do not all of you know Punic." It is to be regretted that he has not left us the exact words of the original. But the Latin generally current was probably much on a par with the English spoken on the Gold Coast or in Sierra Leone; and the style of some inscriptions which have been preserved is not much more correct, if perhaps less ambitious, than that of the native newspapers written in English.† Augustine himself,

* See Cust, *Modern Languages of Africa*, i. 82.

† I cannot refrain from quoting in illustration a poem which appeared some years ago in a Sierra Leone periodical. I need hardly say that it is perfectly serious.

"O bellum, what a name!
That enemy of peace!
Horror spreads his fame,
That banisher of bliss;
He works such desolation,
And brings sad contemplation,
And fearful ruination,
And endless separation.

though he had had a University education at Carthage, found, even after spending some years in Italy, that Italians laughed at him for his pronunciation (*adhuc in multis verborum sonis Itali exagitant*). It is interesting also to read what M. Gaston Boissier says * about the Latin written by two other African provincials, Apuleius (best remembered for the tale of Cupid and Psyche to which, so far as is known, he was the first to give literary form) and the Christian poet Dracontius.

Traces of the Roman occupation remain in the "Berber" language. The dialect used in the Aures Mountains is, says Cust, "full of Latin words . . . they call a garden **orta,** an elm **olm :** the New Year's salutation is **Boniné** or 'Bonus Annus.' They use the solar year, and the names of their months **Yenar, Mars, Maio, Yunio,** are obviously borrowed from the Latin."

Punic, as we have said, has long been extinct, and has left no traces beyond inscriptions. It is otherwise with Arabic, which may be said to have come into Africa by two distinct routes; first, by the Moslem conquest of the north, and, secondly, by the colonisation of the east coast.

About the eighteenth year of the Muhammadan era—that is, in A.D. 639—Amr, a lieutenant of the second Caliph, Omar, invaded Egypt; and, by the end of the century, the Arab hosts had overrun the whole of North Africa, as far as the Atlantic, and even crossed into Spain. The old Gothic kingdom was conquered in a very short time,

---

Where'er his course he runs
What havoc he doth wrought,
The civil, savage turns,
The savage turns to brute,
The parents become childless,
And happy wives turn widows,
The children become homeless,
That's war where'er he goes!"

* *L'Afrique Romaine*, pp. 272–314.

and so would France have been if Charles Martel had not defeated the "Saracens" at Tours in 729.

The Berbers resisted the invaders for a time, at first under their chief Kuseila, after his death under a queen, Dihia-al-Kahina. She was killed in battle in 705, and the Berbers, having become converts to Islam (a process effected without much difficulty) settled down (at least comparatively speaking) under their new rulers. There were other invasions during the eleventh century, which, Sir H. H. Johnston says,* "have been the main source of the Arab element in the northern part of the continent." Without them, he thinks, "Muhammadanism might have faded away, and a series of independent Berber states have been formed once more under Christian rule."

The ultimate outcome was the rise of the four "Barbary States"—Tripoli, Tunis, Algiers and Morocco—which long remained a danger to European commerce and the lives and liberties of European travellers. At present only Morocco retains a nominal independence. To enter further into their past history or present conditions would be foreign to the purpose of this book; the only point we have to notice is that they represent Arab domination over a Hamitic race, and that the Arabic language is spoken throughout their area, if not by all (or nearly all) their inhabitants. It has also been carried across the Sahara by the caravans which have come and gone to Timbuktu since the dawn of history, and people able to speak Arabic may be found scattered through most parts of West Africa, while the Arabic words which have found their way into Songhai, Hausa, Fula and other languages testify to its widespread influence.

People who have adopted Islam naturally borrow the Arabic religious phraseology. The Koran is never translated (that being held an unlawful act), but learnt by heart

* *The Colonisation of Africa*, p. 17.

in the original and afterwards explained in the vernacular to those able and willing to carry their studies any further.

It should be added that Arabic is now spoken throughout Egypt (having quite displaced Coptic, the direct descendant of Old Egyptian, which is now only used in the liturgical books of the Egyptian Christians), and has spread southward through the Sudan. A very corrupt form of it is spoken by the "Sudanese" troops in the Uganda Protectorate.

The Arab settlements on the east coast were of a more unobtrusive and peaceful character. The earliest is believed to have been that of the island of Pate (the largest of the Lamu Archipelago) where the Sultanate, founded in 689 A.D. lasted well into the nineteenth century. The Arabs at one time occupied trading stations on the Zambezi and even south of it, at Sofala, but the Portuguese soon ousted them from these and retained possession of them, though they failed to keep their hold on Mombasa and Malindi.

The influence of Arabic on Swahili has already been noticed in the chapter on the Bantu languages. The latter is the general medium of communication, and Arabic itself, though kept up among themselves by people of good position and by the Shehri and other recent immigrants from Arabia, and officially used by the Sultan of Zanzibar and his court, is of less immediate importance than in North Africa and Egypt.

As already stated, the character is used by educated natives in writing Swahili. It is not very well adapted for this purpose, as it does not provide for all the Bantu sounds—less so, in fact, than our Roman alphabet, defective as it is. But as the number of people who use it in correspondence is far from inconsiderable, every one likely to have dealings with the coast people would be well advised to learn it. There is also a certain amount of Swahili poetry written in this character, some of it, perhaps, of a respectable age, which still awaits examination. It seems doubtful, at present, if there are any prose MSS. except those written quite recently. Older MSS., if any exist, are probably (like the Chronicle of Kilwa published in the *Journal of the Royal Asiatic Society* for 1895) in Arabic.

The principal Semitic languages, I need hardly say, are *written* languages. The general look of Hebrew and Arabic letters is known to every one; but two points should be specially noticed; they are written from *right to left*, and *the vowels are left out*, as in Pitman's Shorthand. If absolutely necessary, they are put in above or below the letter which they follow; but "pointed books" (that is, with the vowel-points inserted) are, both in Hebrew and Arabic, a concession to the weakness of the beginner. When Swahili is written in the Arabic character, the vowel-points are indispensable, because not even a native can always tell, without them, what a word is meant to be. Arabic expressions (such as the complimentary formulæ which begin and end a letter) are always, on the other hand, left unpointed. The Phœnician writing, which, on the whole, resembles the Hebrew, shares with it this characteristic. We know it from inscriptions discovered in Palestine, North Africa and elsewhere; and it has this special interest that it is supposed to be the immediate parent of the Greek and Roman alphabets, the latter of which we use to this day. The very earliest Greek inscriptions are supposed to have been written from right to left, like the Phœnician; at a later date the style called *Boustrophedon* * was adopted, in which the writing runs alternately to right and left, turning at the end of the line, like the furrows in a ploughed field. The laws of Solon were inscribed on tablets after this fashion, in the sixth century B.C. It gradually gave place to the method now used for all European languages,

* Literally "ox turning."

though the old style was sometimes purposely kept up, in the inscriptions on vases, etc.

The Amharic character, unlike those just referred to, is written from left to right: it also has another important difference: each character is not a letter in our sense, but stands for a syllable. The same character, with slight modifications to indicate the difference of vowel, represents *ba, be, bi, bo, bu* or *da, de, di, do, du*. Thus it is evident that a much larger number of signs is required than in Hebrew or Arabic, while, on the other hand, there is no inconvenience arising from the absence of vowel symbols.

The cuneiform writing of the Babylonian tablets is also syllabic, and reads from left to right. It is interesting to remember that it does not really belong to the Semitic Assyrians, who used it to write their language much as the Swahili use the Arabic script, but was taken over by them from the Sumerians, whose language is of an entirely different type.

We have already seen that the Semitic and Hamitic languages have various features in common, but one great distinction between them is the existence of what are called *triliteral roots* in the former. That is to say that the root of a verb (which is found in the third person singular of the "perfect" tense) normally consists of three consonants, as in the Arabic **qatala** "he killed," **nasara** "he helped," and the Hebrew **lamad** "he learnt," **nathan** "he gave." Verbs consisting of more than three consonants are either "derived forms" or of a later formation; those with only two radicals are probably contracted. These triliteral roots seem to be quite peculiar to the Semitic family.

The "derived forms" of verbs (also called "aspects," "species" or "conjugations") familiar to all who have studied Hebrew or Arabic, are found, as we have seen, both in the Hamitic and in the Bantu languages; in the latter, I venture to think, their function and meaning are most clearly exhibited. In Hebrew there are seven conjugations; in Arabic fifteen, though some of them are very seldom used. The difficulty felt in defining the exact force of these conjugations suggests that they are an old formation gradually losing its significance, and a study of the Bantu verb makes the matter far more comprehensible.

There are properly only two tenses, and these are not *tenses* as we understand the word, *i.e.*, exact indications of *time*, past, present or future; they only mark *complete* and *incomplete action*. This, as all students of Hebrew know, is one of the great difficulties connected with that language, underlying many vexed questions in the interpretation of the Old Testament Scriptures.

The *Perfect* tense indicates difference of person by *suffixes*, the *Imperfect* (sometimes called "future") by *prefixes* in some cases combined with a change of termination.

There are two genders, masculine and feminine (extending to the second and third persons of verbs) and three numbers: singular, dual and plural.

Both in Hebrew and Arabic we find what are called anomalous plurals, masculine nouns taking a feminine termination in the plural, and *vice versâ*.

"Some masculine substantives have a plural of the feminine form in *-ôth*, and *vice versâ* some feminines a plural of the masculine form, in *îm*. . . . Such, for instance, are **abh** "father," plural **abhôth**, **yônah** "dove," plural **yônîm**" (*Arnold's First Hebrew Book*).

Such nouns are in most grammars dismissed as "exceptions," a term which usually means that the rule has not been discovered or is not understood. Probably they are survivals from an older stage of the language in which most, if not all, plurals were governed by the Law of Polarity, as shown in the last chapter.

The structure of the Semitic languages is—even apart

from their literature, of which nothing can be said here—full of interest; but these few general indications are all that is needed for our present purpose, which is merely to show the extent of ground occupied by them in Africa and the relation in which they stand to the remaining African families.

The only ones of any practical importance from our point of view are Amharic, which must be learnt by any one whose work takes him to Abyssinia, and Arabic, which, of course, is needed in Egypt and throughout North Africa, including the Sudan.

In this necessarily brief and imperfect survey, enough has, I think, been said to furnish, as it were, a general outline or map of the subject as a guide to further study.

The appended Bibliography is not intended to be exhaustive, only to give a list of the most important works, with a few notes as to the way in which they will be found most useful.

It is needless to dwell on the value of language as a key to the psychology of a race; and the day is long past when the study of "barbarous jargons" was considered, at best, a harmless sort of craze. This book makes no attempt to discuss the deeper problems of philology; but I cannot forbear calling attention, once more, to the strong probability that further research into these languages may throw some additional light on what was once deemed an impenetrable mystery—the origin of speech.

I have in the course of these pages referred to the late Dean Farrar's *Language and Languages*, an interesting and suggestive work, even if parts of it are now out of date. (His view of the onomatopoetic and interjectional origin of language is really sounder than Max Müller's, and every fresh discovery tends to confirm it.) I must recur to it once more in order to illustrate my concluding remarks. The concluding chapter, on the "Allophylian languages" (quite a reasonable and adequate term at the time of writing) contains a great deal which, were the writer living to-day, he would see reason to modify. It is pervaded by the conception of the savage-in-the-abstract, that terrible and loathly being who loomed large in European consciousness about the middle of last century, but whose lineaments tend to become faint and vague in the light of closer acquaintance with real Zulus and Veddahs and Inuits, all differing from each other, and some, perhaps, highly objectionable, but none exactly like the type-picture. But, passing this by, we find Farrar saying of these people that their languages, "rich in words for all that can be eaten or handled, seem absolutely incapable of expressing the reflex conceptions of the intellect, or the higher forms of the consciousness; . . . peoples whose tongues in some instances have twenty names for murder, but no name for love, no name for gratitude, no name for God. . . . Is it not clear that, in such a language as this * all literary culture, all refined expression, all elevated teaching are impossible?"

However, it is not fair to omit the next sentence, for, wide of the mark as are the author's premises, his conclusion is most unexceptionable:

"Yet both the Hindoos and we have suffered terribly, and still are suffering more seriously, for our neglect and contempt of these primitive populations."

But our main point is that, had he not been dominated by the Abstract Savage—and perhaps also by the rush of his own eloquence—he would have seen that he was virtually contradicting what he himself had written elsewhere, more especially in the chapters on "Metaphor." What are the

* The Khasia, of Assam, as to which, not being acquainted with it, I can express no opinion.

most abstract terms of the most highly cultivated languages, in the last resort, but very material metaphors? **Spiritus** means "breath" and **umoya**, in Zulu, means "breath"; but it is also used for "spirit" in any of the higher senses, and is so understood by all Christian Zulus. The truth is that language expands with the intellectual growth of a people, and there is no reason why Zulu or Swahili (whose *present* capacity, moreover, is too apt to be underrated) should not some day be the vehicle of a literature worthy to stand beside those of the older world.

Whether the people themselves are capable of developing is another question and one often too readily answered in the negative; in any case it cannot be considered here.

Neither can we dwell on the many interesting problems connected with the movements and changes of language, the disuse of one, the adoption of another (as the Wasanye speak Galla and the Dorobo Masai), the modifications produced by contact with foreign speech (*e.g.*, the Arabic influence in Hausa and Swahili) or, in the adopted one through assimilation to native idioms, as in the English of Sierra Leone, the French of Mauritius and the "Afrikandertaal" of the Cape. How far can language be influenced by conscious effort of the individual? A missionary introduces a new word—it may "catch on" and gain currency, or it may rapidly pass into oblivion. These and many other points suggest themselves for consideration; but one thing must be steadily kept in view: language is a living thing, which must grow and change, which cannot be forced into a dead mechanical framework, and which no human efforts, though they may to some extent modify it, can either create or destroy.

BIBLIOGRAPHY

I: General Philology

T. G. Tucker, *Introduction to the Natural History of Language.* London (Blackie and Sons), 1908.

O. Jespersen, *Language: its Nature, Development and Origin.* London (George Allen and Unwin), 1922.

H. Sweet, *The History of Language.* London (Dent), 1899.

Either this or one of the two following will be found an excellent introduction to the subject, which should be followed up, if practicable, by the larger works of Tucker and Jespersen.

E. Sapir, *Language: an Introduction to the Study of Speech.* Oxford University Press, 1921.

E. H. Sturtevant, *Linguistic Change: an Introduction to the Historical Study of Language.* Chicago (University Press), 1917.

R. N. Cust, *Modern Languages of Africa,* 2 vols. London (Kegan Paul and Co.), 1883.

Sufficient has been said in the text to indicate the scope and limitations of this work. It has not yet been superseded.

C. Meinhof (trans. A. Werner), *An Introduction to the Study of African Languages* (*Moderne Sprachforschung in Afrika*). London (Dent), 1915.

The article "Philology," in the latest edition of the *Encyclopædia Britannica* is full of valuable information in a highly compressed form, and gives numerous references to special works. The Bibliography for Missionary Students, published by the Board of Study for the Preparation of Missionaries,* will be found a useful guide to recent literature, and is kept up-to-date by supplements appearing three times a year.

II: Phonetics

The Principles of the International Phonetic Association. A pamphlet, first published in 1912, and to be obtained from Professor D. Jones, University College. Price 3s.

G. Noël-Armfield, *General Phonetics for Missionaries and Students of Languages.* 2nd edition. Cambridge (Heffer and Sons), 1919.

D. Jones, *An Outline of English Phonetics.* Leipzig (Teubner).

III: Sudan Languages

D. Westermann, *Die Sudansprachen.* Hamburg, 1911.

Contains numerous references to books dealing with particular languages.

Unfortunately not yet translated into English. As pointed out in the notes, the recent researches of Mr N. W. Thomas and Dr Struck have shown that the classification adopted in this work is not exhaustive, but no comprehensive survey of the remaining West

* Inquiries should be addressed to the Secretary, Edinburgh House, 2, Eaton Gate London, S.W.1.

African languages will be possible for some time to come. Professor Westermann has also published (in German) a Grammar and Dictionary of Ewe, and, in English:

Grammar and Vocabulary of the Shilluk Language.

The Shilluk People, Language, and Folk-Lore. London (Kegan Paul), 1912.

Both these last are of the greatest value to anyone working on the White Nile.

A. B. Ellis, *The Tshi-speaking Peoples of the Gold Coast.* 1887.

A. B. Ellis, *The Ewe-speaking Peoples of the Slave Coast.* 1890.

A. B. Ellis, *The Yoruba-speaking Peoples of the Slave Coast.* 1894.

These three books (originally published by Chapman and Hall, but now out of print and very scarce) are valuable for the insight they give into the structure of the languages, and also from the anthropological point of view. They should be supplemented by Captain R. S. Rattray's special work, *Ashanti* (Oxford University Press, 1922).

Sir H. H. Johnston, *Liberia.* London (Hutchinson), 1906.

The chapters on Language (Vol. II, xxxi and xxxiii) are interesting and important in this connection.

IV: Bantu Languages

W. H. I. Bleek, *A Comparative Grammar of South African Bantu Languages.* London (Kegan Paul and Co.). Part I, 1862; Part II, 1869.

Still extremely valuable, but the student is advised not to embark on it before acquiring some knowledge of phonetics (pp. 11–92, more especially, will need to be checked by the latest results obtained in that science) and read, at least, Meinhof's *Moderne Sprachforschung.*

C. Meinhof, *Grundzüge einer vergleichenden Grammatik der Bantusprachen.* Berlin (D. Reimer), 1906.

C. Meinhof, *Grundriss einer Lautlehre der Bantusprachen.* Second edition. Same Publisher, 1910.

W. Bourquin, *Neue Bantuwortstämme.* Same Publisher, 1923.

The author has compiled a list of stems common to a large number of Bantu languages, and attempted to give the hypothetical ground-forms. The meaning of each is given in English as well as in German, thus adding to the usefulness of the book, which embodies some of the material contained in Meinhof's *Lautlehre.*

Sir H. H. Johnston, *A Comparative Study of the Bantu and Semi-Bantu Languages,* 2 vols. Oxford University Press, 1919–22.

See also the same author's article, "Bantu Languages," in the latest edition of the *Encyclopædia Britannica.*

A. Werner, *Introductory Sketch of the Bantu Languages.* London (Kegan Paul), 1919

V: Hamitic Languages

C. Meinhof, *Die Sprachen der Hamiten.* Hamburg (Friedrichsen), 1912.

Almost, if not quite, the only special work available, but the *Encyclopædia Britannica* article, "Hamitic Races and Languages," should be consulted. For the early history of Egypt and its connection with the other early civilizations of the Mediterranean and Western Asia, see

J. H. Breasted, *Ancient Times: a History of the Early World.* Boston, U.S.A. (Ginn and Co.), 1916.

J. H. Breasted, *History of Egypt,* second edition. London, 1920.

H. R. Hall, *Ancient History of the Near East,* second edition. 1920.

VI: The Bushman Languages

To the references given in the notes to this chapter may be added a further instalment of material recently published by Dr Bleek's daughter:

Dorothea Bleek, *The Mantis and his Friends.* Cape Town (Maskew Miller), 1923.

Miss Bleek's introductory chapter gives a great deal of general information about the Bushmen.

VII: Semitic Languages

Prof. Nöldeke's article in the *Encyclopædia Britannica* gives a very good general survey. The French edition of Brockelmann's Comparative Grammar (*Précis de Linguistique Sémitique*, traduit par W. Marçais et M. Cohen, Paris (P. Geuthner, 1910) is an excellent introduction to the subject. For general information, G. A. Barton, *A Sketch of Semitic Origins, Social and Religious*, New York, 1902, may be recommended, and, for more advanced readers, Robertson Smith's *Religion of the Semites.*

NOTES AND CORRECTIONS

Page 21. See note on Chapter III.

Page 26, note. The etymology of the word "Hottentot" is far from certain. It may, as Dr Struck has pointed out (*Archiv für Anthropologie,* 1920, p. 78) be of native origin, as De La Loubère, a French traveller, who visited the Cape in 1687 or 1688, says that the word "hotantot" was continually repeated in the songs which accompanied their dances, and that this was why they were called Hottentots.

Chapter III, pp. 34–50. This chapter requires some modification. Westermann's conclusions, sound as far as they go, apply to a smaller number of languages than at first seemed probable. There are others which will not fit the definition given on p. 36—the position of the genitive, for instance, varies considerably. There are at least three distinct groups of what are now classed as "Semi-Bantu" languages, including, for instance, Ekoi and Efik (Calabar), Avatime (Togo), Temne and Bulom (Sierra Leone). Sir Harry Johnston thinks they are more likely to be independent offshoots from a pre-Bantu stock than degenerate Bantu idioms. It would be premature to attempt an exhaustive classification of West African languages, but the reader is referred to a paper on "The Sudanic Languages," by Mr N. W. Thomas, published in the Bulletin of the School of Oriental Studies, Vol. I, Part IV (1920), pp. 16–124.

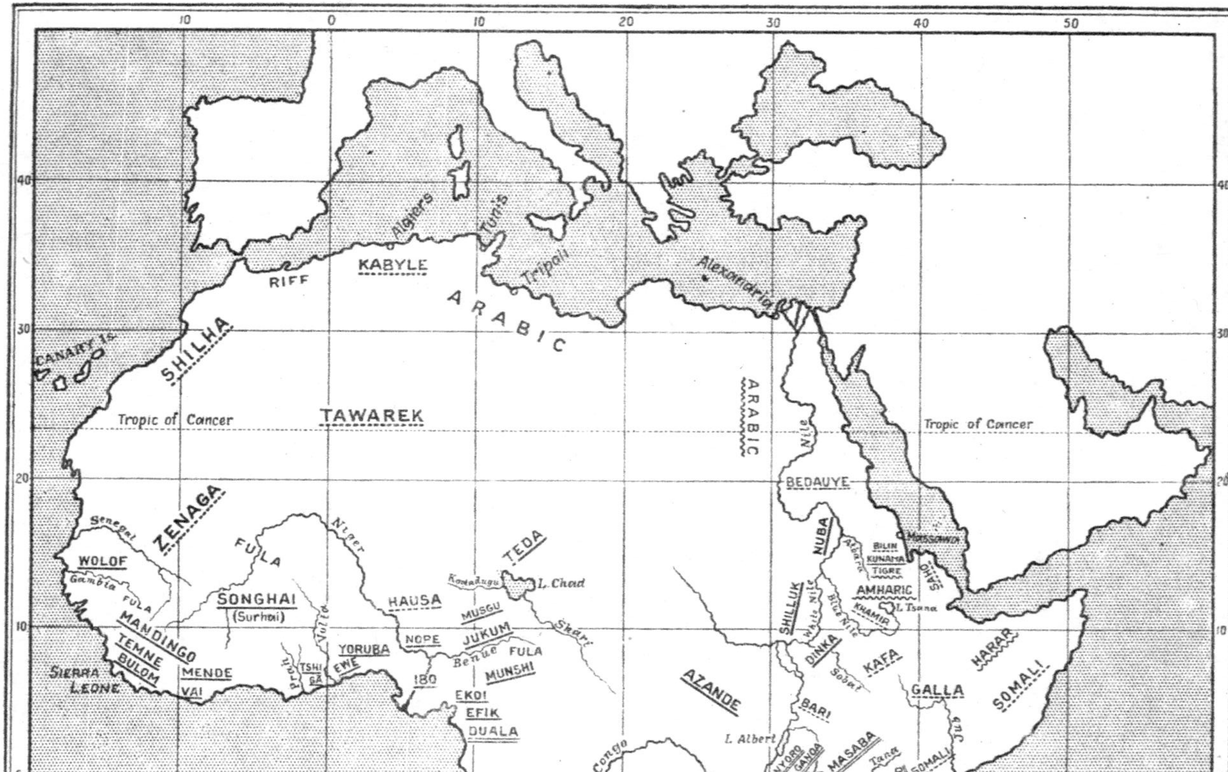

KABYLE
RIFF
Algiers
Tunis
Tripoli
Alexandria
ARABIC
SHILHA
CANARY Is.
Tropic of Cancer
TAWAREK
ARABIC
Nile
BEDAUYE
Tropic of Cancer
ZENAGA
Senegal
WOLOF
Gambia
FULA
FULA
SONGHAI
(Surhai)
MANDINGO
TEMNE
BULOM
SIERRA LEONE
MENDE
VAI
Niger
Volta
Prah
TSHI
GÃ
EWE
YORUBA
HAUSA
NOPE
IBO
TEDA
L. Chad
MUSGU
JUKUM
Benue
FULA
MUNSHI
EKOI
EFIK
DUALA
Shari
AZANDE
Congo
L. Albert
NUBA
SHILLUK
White Nile
Blue Nile
Atbara
BILIN
KUNAMA
TIGRE
Massawa
SAHO
AMHARIC
KHAMIR
L. Tsana
DINKA
Sobat
KAFA
BARI
NYORO
GANDA
MASABA
Tana
SOMALI
Jub
GALLA
HARAR
SOMALI

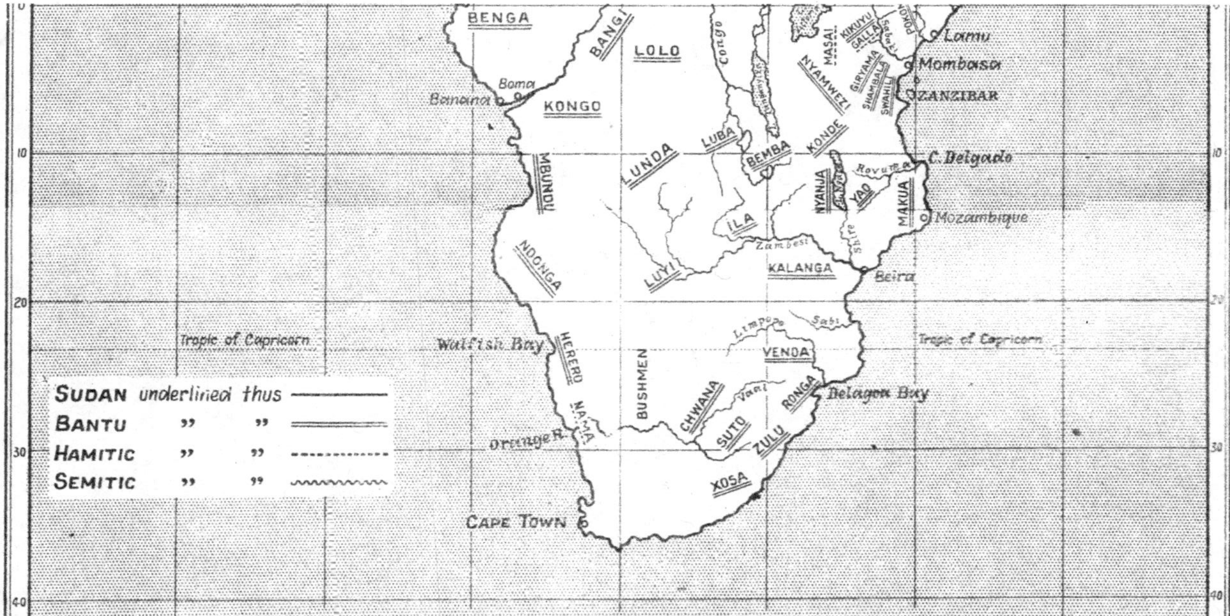

A MAP TO ILLUSTRATE "THE LANGUAGE FAMILIES OF AFRICA"

[To face p. 150.

Page 61. The last foot-note should read: "This class, in Swahili, loses its prefix altogether. It is not correct to say, as is done in some grammars, that, when the stem begins with a vowel, it takes the prefix *j* (*jino*, *jicho*, *jina*): the *j* stands for the original initial consonant (probably γ), represented in Zulu by *z*, which is dropped in the plural (*meno* being contracted from *ma-ino*).

Page 63 (foot-notes). It seems clear that there existed, originally, both an augmentative and a depreciative class, which, in many cases, have not survived at all. Where they are discoverable at the present day, it is not always easy to distinguish them. *Gu* in Ganda, seems to include both meanings. The *ga*-prefix, serving as plural to *gu*- in Ganda, has not been found anywhere else, and Professor Meinhof declines to recognise it as a distinct class.

Chapter VI, p. 100. This chapter, which is mainly condensed from Meinhof and Westermann, has been criticized with some freedom by recent students of Fulani. As, however, I am by no means convinced that the views there set forth have been effectively refuted, and as correction in points of detail (which I gladly acknowledge to be necessary) is impossible in this edition, I have decided to let it stand—only remarking that the text on pp. 113, 114 cannot, it seems, be accepted as a satisfactory specimen of Fulani.